Reconfiguring Pakistan Econ

There has been a great deal of speculation and prognostication about the China-Pakistan Economic Corridor (CPEC). The project's name suggests it is intended to be an 'economic corridor' connecting Pakistan overland with China's Xinjiang province. This book examines whether CPEC's primary purpose is as an overland conduit for trade and economic cooperation between China and Pakistan. The key finding is that aims related to regional geopolitics and internal security have, in reality, a more significant impact.

The book demonstrates that China's goals in Pakistan are primarily geopolitical rather than geo-economic, since the notion of constructing an economic and transportation 'corridor' between Pakistan and China is logistically and economically problematic due to a range of foreseeable problems. Most importantly, border disputes with India and the containment of domestic separatism motivate are the driving forces for cooperation between the partners.

This book will be of interest to scholars who research the BRI, as well as policy makers.

Jeremy Garlick, PhD, is an associate professor at Prague University of Economics and Business and the director of the Jan Masaryk Centre of International Studies, a research centre within the university. He specialises in China's international relations, focusing primarily on the progress and regional implementation of the Belt and Road Initiative (BRI). His first book, *The Impact of China's Belt and Road Initiative: From Asia to Europe*, was published by Routledge in 2020. In addition to publications on EU-China relations, he has also published numerous articles on a diverse range of topics related to the BRI, including China's economic diplomacy and regionalising foreign policy. These publications include papers on the China-Pakistan Economic Corridor (CPEC), China's economic diplomacy in the Czech Republic, China's strategic hedging in the Persian Gulf, China's normative power drive in Central Asia, and China's relations with India. Dr Garlick has taught and lectured for two decades at institutes of higher education in Asia and Europe, including the University of the Chinese Academy of Sciences (UCAS) in Beijing and Ewha Womans University in Seoul.

Routledge Frontiers of Political Economy

Political Economy of Financialization in the United States
A Historical – Institutional Balance-Sheet Approach
Kurt Mettenheim

The International Political Economy of the Renminbi
Currency Internationalization and Reactive Currency Statecraft
Hyoung-kyu Chey

Explaining Wealth Inequality
Property, Possession and Policy Reform
Benedict Atkinson

The International Political Economy of the Renminbi
Currency Internationalization and Reactive Currency Statecraft
Hyoung-kyu Chey

Financialization of the Economy, Business, and Household Inequality in the United States
A Historical – Institutional Balance-Sheet Approach
Kurt Mettenheim with Olivier Butzbach

Economic Ideas, Policy and National Culture
A Comparison of Three Market Economies
Edited by Eelke de Jong

Political Economy of Contemporary Italy
The Economic Crisis and State Intervention
Nicolò Giangrande

Reconfiguring the China-Pakistan Economic Corridor
Geo-Economic Pipe Dreams Versus Geopolitical Realities
Jeremy Garlick

For more information about this series, please visit: www.routledge.com/Routledge-Frontiers-of-Political-Economy/book-series/SE0345

Reconfiguring the China-Pakistan Economic Corridor

Geo-Economic Pipe Dreams Versus Geopolitical Realities

Jeremy Garlick

Funding details: This work was supported by the Czech Science Foundation (Grantová Agentura České Republiky, GAČR), as part of the research project 'China's multifaceted economic diplomacy in the era of the Belt and Road Initiative', project no. 19–01809S.

Routledge
Taylor & Francis Group
LONDON AND NEW YORK

First published 2022
by Routledge
2 Park Square, Milton Park, Abingdon, Oxon OX14 4RN

and by Routledge
605 Third Avenue, New York, NY 10158

Routledge is an imprint of the Taylor & Francis Group, an informa business

British Library Cataloguing-in-Publication Data
A catalogue record for this book is available from the British Library

Library of Congress Cataloging-in-Publication Data
Names: Garlick, Jeremy, author.
Title: Reconfiguring the China-Pakistan economic corridor : geo-economic pipe dreams versus geopolitical realities / Jeremy Garlick.
Description: Abingdon, Oxon ; New York, NY : Routledge, 2022. | Series: Frontiers of political economy | Includes bibliographical references and index.
Identifiers: LCCN 2021030729 | ISBN 9780367863210 (hardback) | ISBN 9781032151861 (paperback) | ISBN 9781003018377 (ebook)
Subjects: LCSH: China—Foreign economic relations—Pakistan. | Pakistan—Foreign economic relations—China. | Economic development—Political aspects—Pakistan. | Geopolitics—China.
Classification: LCC HF1604.Z4 P3543 2022 | DDC 337.5105491—dc23
LC record available at https://lccn.loc.gov/2021030729

ISBN: 978-0-367-86321-0 (hbk)
ISBN: 978-1-032-15186-1 (pbk)
ISBN: 978-1-003-01837-7 (ebk)

DOI: 10.4324/9781003018377

Typeset in Galliard
by Apex CoVantage, LLC

Contents

Figures

Maps

Tables

Acknowledgements

This book would not have been possible without the input of Lam Yongling, my editor at Routledge, who first suggested that I write it. Her encouragement has been the spur to complete the manuscript. Editorial assistant Payal Bharti has provided invaluable assistance throughout the writing process. Without their help, I would not have finished the book.

A debt is also owed to Professor Suisheng Zhao of Denver University, the editor of *Journal of Contemporary China*. It was his decision to publish the article which was the foundation for this book. Whatever standing I have as an authority on China-Pakistan relations rests on that decision.

I very much appreciate the continued support of members of the Faculty of International Relations of Prague University of Economics and Business, especially Josef Taušer, Štěpánka Zemanová, and Radka Druláková. Their guidance and trust have helped me to maintain focus and sustain the energy to complete this and other research tasks. Invaluable assistance in locating Chinese-language articles on CPEC was provided by Qin Fangxing. She also helped me with understanding various nuances in the texts at crucial junctures.

My final thanks go to my family, who have waited patiently while I tapped away at my keyboard in the corner of the room. Their willingness to put up with the long hours I have spent at the computer has enabled me finally to fall over the line and present you with the volume you hold in your hands, whatever its ultimate value might turn out to be.

Abbreviations

BBC	British Broadcasting Corporation
BLA	Baloch Liberation Army
BRI	Belt and Road Initiative
CASCF	China-Arab States Cooperation Forum
CCP	Chinese Communist Party
CEE	Central and Eastern Europe
CEFC	CEFC China Energy Company Limited
CHEC	China Harbor Engineering Company
CIA	Central Intelligence Agency
COPHC	China Overseas Ports Holding Company
COVID	Coronavirus disease (COVID-19)
CPEC	China-Pakistan Economic Corridor
DWT	Deadweight tonnage
ETIM	East Turkestan Islamic Movement
FOCAC	Forum on China-Africa Cooperation
GDP	Gross domestic product
IMF	International Monetary Fund
IOR	Indian Ocean region
IR	International Relations
JCPOA	Joint Comprehensive Plan of Action (Iran nuclear deal)
KPK	Khyber Pakhtunkhwa
ML-1	Mainline-1 (Karachi/Lahore/Peshawar railway link)
MW	Megawatts
NDRC	National Development and Reform Commission
NWFP	North-West Frontier Province
PC	Project cycle
PLA	People's Liberation Army
PLAN	People's Liberation Army Navy
PPP	Pakistan People's Party
PRC	People's Republic of China
PSA	Port of Singapore Authority
PTI	Pakistan Tehreek-e-Insaf party
RMB	Renminbi (official name of Chinese currency)

SCO	Shanghai Cooperation Organization
SLOC	Sea lines of communication
SREB	Silk Road Economic Belt
TAPI	Turkmenistan-Afghanistan-Pakistan-India pipeline
UN	United Nations
XUAR	Xinjiang Uyghur Autonomous Region

1 Introduction

Higher than the Himalayas, deeper than the ocean?

> *Higher than the Himalayas, deeper than the ocean, and sweeter than honey* – A slogan frequently used (with slight variations) by Pakistani and Chinese leaders to describe the relationship between the two countries – supposedly first uttered by Premier Zhou Enlai in 1964.
>
> (Khan 2021)

1.1 The 'logic' of the China-Pakistan Economic Corridor

In April 2015, during a visit by President Xi Jinping, agreements for $46 billion of Chinese infrastructure investments in Pakistan were signed (Yao 2015: 36). The investments were intended to finance new energy and transportation infrastructure in Pakistan intended to develop what was to be called the 'China-Pakistan Economic Corridor' (CPEC). Apart from providing the financing, China would also instruct its companies to build the planned infrastructure. The principal idea, reportedly based on the suggestion of former Pakistani President Pervez Musharraf 13 years earlier (Lu 2014/2015: 165; Markey 2020: vii; Boni 2020: 82), was to connect the province of Xinjiang in northwest China with the port of Gwadar, strategically located on the Indian Ocean. The implied intention was to create an overland trade route across Pakistan so that Chinese imports – especially oil – and exports could be transported by a shorter, supposedly more secure route than the maritime one via the Straits of Malacca and the South China Sea. Subsequently, in 2017, it was announced that the amount of promised Chinese investments had increased to $62 billion (Siddiqui 2017) – a highly significant sum of money for impoverished, debt-ridden Pakistan.

Accordingly, most observers, basing their conclusions on the enthusiastic presentations delivered by Pakistani leaders, interpreted the primary goal of CPEC to be the construction of overland connectivity infrastructure between China and Pakistan. An extraordinary amount of ink was spilt to explain that a new pipeline would carry oil from Gwadar to Kashgar.[1] The pipeline would neatly overcome the 'Malacca dilemma' – the risk of Chinese fuel supplies being impacted by a blockade in times of crisis, presumably by the US navy, and generating positive outcomes for China's energy security. Some commentators hastened to point out

DOI: 10.4324/9781003018377-1

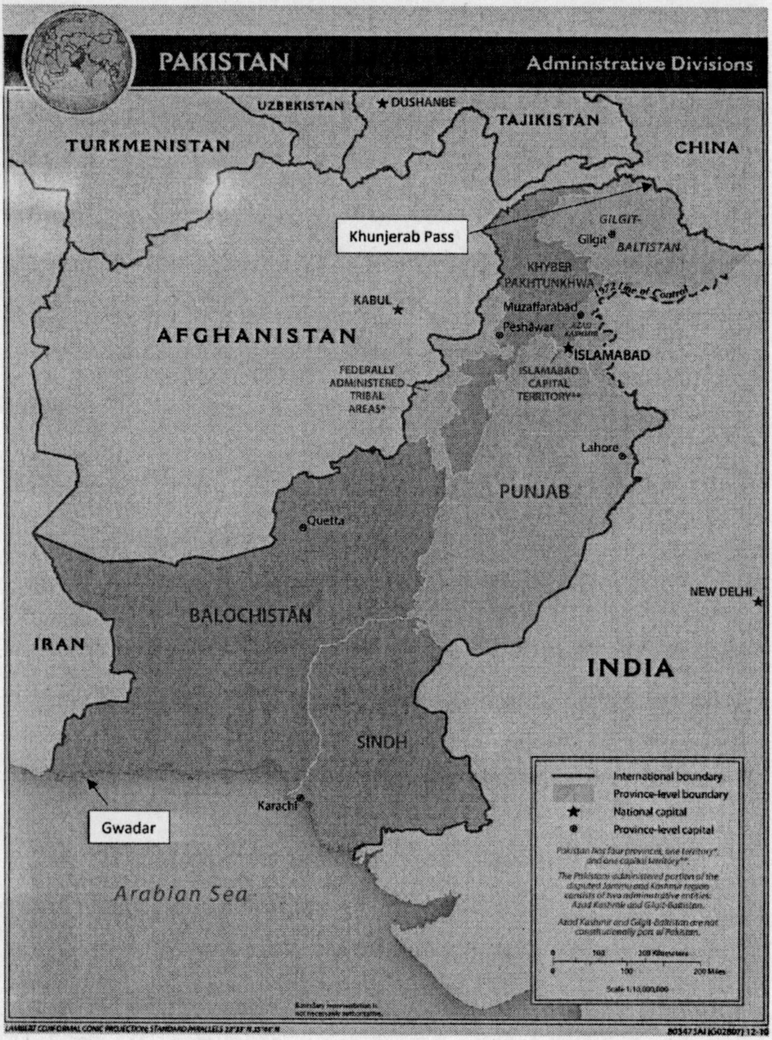

that it would also supposedly be cheaper and quicker to transport oil by this shorter route, even including calculations which purported to demonstrate the economic and time advantages available (Alam et al 2019). In addition, even though no cross-border railway project has ever been officially endorsed and no feasibility study or plan has ever been published, some Chinese scholars assumed that a trans-Himalayan railway was an integral part of the megaproject and that the planning process was under way (Cheng 2015: 98; Zhao and Liu 2017: 123). The 'economic corridor' part of the CPEC name was thus taken literally as a set of construction projects design to enhance the already-existing overland connection between the two countries.

On the Pakistani side, CPEC was standardly lauded as an economic 'game changer', using a slogan seemingly introduced by Prime Minister Nawaz Sharif in the lead-up to the megaproject's official launch (Ahmar 2015: 48). Officials, the media, and even scholars fell into line behind this slogan. With Chinese assistance, Pakistan would be able to develop faster. New industries would emerge. Jobs would be created. Pakistan's energy crisis – many households still lack electricity and blackouts are frequent – would be solved. The enhanced overland connection with China would produce win-win synergies which would generate economic benefits for the Uyghurs of Xinjiang province as well as Pakistani citizens. When CPEC was finally included in China's Belt and Road Initiative (BRI) as a 'flagship project', it seemed that it was only a matter of time before economic synergies would be generated by connecting the Indian Ocean with Central Asia.

Thus, even before the official launch of CPEC, a set of very specific phrases and narrative conventions had been established to describe the new megaproject. As this book will reveal, stock phrases such as 'Malacca dilemma', 'game changer', and 'flagship project' have become standardised usages in connection with CPEC in much of the scholarly literature, as well as the media. Even the officially endorsed notion of CPEC being an 'economic corridor' from Gwadar to Kashgar presents a very specific image of the megaproject as a trade route connecting the Indian Ocean with the interior of China – but one which does not correspond well with the messy on-the-ground reality. As this book will demonstrate, the progress of CPEC from 2015 to 2020 does not match the image conjured in the public mind by much of the prevailing media and scholarly coverage – an image which persists as received wisdom due to constant repetition.

This book challenges the rather misleading narratives about CPEC which have unfortunately become established in scholarly discourse – as well as in the global media – due to the prevalence of the fixed phrases and concepts outlined in the previous paragraphs, and to replace them with a perspective grounded in the reality of what is happening in Pakistan. The task of deconstructing the established narrative and constructing a new one based on real-world empirics to establish a better understanding of CPEC will be achieved by critically examining the prevailing discourse – academic and official – and locating it against a range of empirical data concerning the megaproject's progress and the partners' motivations. For instance, data concerning Chinese investments obtained from Pakistani and Chinese government sources will be deployed to demonstrate which parts of the established CPEC narrative hold up and which do not. Other empirical evidence concerning international shipping, port construction, oil pipelines, trans-Himalayan transportation routes, and other allegedly important features of CPEC will be obtained from a range of official and independent sources.

While some may object that official sources are not necessarily reliable, the book's argument will demonstrate that much of the information thereby obtained surprisingly does not support the established CPEC narrative. While official sources need to be supplemented by independent ones, in many cases official data dispel CPEC myths with surprising force. The words of Chinese experts will frequently be employed in support of the idea that CPEC is not primarily about trans-Himalayan oil pipelines and railways. Instead, the evidence arrayed in this book will reveal that Chinese activity in Pakistan under the CPEC umbrella is focused on four other goals which are also often mentioned in the scholarly literature but are generally given less emphasis.

First, CPEC is supposed to alleviate Pakistan's energy and economic crises through Chinese investment and other infrastructure construction. As will be shown, energy infrastructure projects – power plants, coal mines, dams, and so on – constitute the largest proportion of CPEC investments by China, with the construction of transportation infrastructure within Pakistan in second place. The Pakistani government is short of cash reserves to fund new projects. Since the killing of Osama bin Laden in 2011 in Pakistan, the United States appears to have lost interest in supplying Pakistan with funds or other support. Given Pakistan's unstable domestic politics and frequent violence, it has also proven difficult to attract other investors. Thus, Chinese investments under the umbrella of CPEC present a vital lifeline to Pakistan's perennially troubled economy. The main point, therefore, is to minimise and mitigate Pakistan's economic weakness rather than to transform it according to the 'game changer' narrative.

Second, CPEC consolidates the two countries' mutual interest in countering India militarily. China fought and won a brief war against India in 1962, while there have been Pakistan-India wars in 1947, 1965, 1971, and 1999. Border skirmishes with Indian troops occur at sporadic but frequent intervals, including several clashes between Chinese and Indian soldiers during 2020. In at least one of these, in June 2020, soldiers on both sides were killed (Reuters 2021). Even the China-Pakistan border through which the only road connecting the two countries passes crosses territory claimed by India but currently occupied by Pakistan. In addition, Pakistan's volatile political scene has been dominated by the military throughout its history, with democratically elected governments ousted by army-led coups at regular intervals. Each Pakistani prime minister is aware of the need to keep the army onside if he or she wishes to keep his position. Thus, it is not surprising that the chairman of the CPEC Authority from November 2019 to August 2021 was a retired Pakistani three-star general called Asim Saleem Bajwa. CPEC, like other aspects of China-Pakistan cooperation, involves close coordination between the two countries' military leaders as they seek to consolidate their position in the face of their mutual rival India.

Third, CPEC is supposed to steadily strengthen China's long-term geostrategic position in South Asia and the Indian Ocean by increasing the Chinese presence and influence in Pakistan. Gwadar port, it is frequently repeated, is for commercial purposes, specifically maritime trade. Yet a Bloomberg investigation revealed that in early 2021 there were still only three berths available in the port, none of which were occupied by commercial vessels and at one of which a Pakistani military ship was docked (Bloomberg News 2021). In the absence of significant commercial activity thus far, it is more likely that Gwadar, which China has obtained a long-term lease to develop, will be used as a base from which China will be able to protect its interests in the Indian Ocean and Persian Gulf: Gwadar is situated near the crucial Strait of Hormuz, through which pass significant supplies of oil bound for China. The development of the port of Gwadar, a key CPEC project, allows China to establish a position on the Indian Ocean for use in case of unknown future contingencies in the Indian Ocean region, including ones which require the use of military vessels.

And fourth, CPEC serves to consolidate the ongoing counter-insurgency efforts by both China and Pakistan against internal separatist movements. In China's case, the issue with which it needs Pakistani cooperation is to ensure that there is little or no cross-border support for the Uyghur separatist movement in Xinjiang. By cooperating closely with the Pakistani army, the Chinese government and its People's Liberation Army (PLA) hope to ensure that assistance does not find its way to the Uyghurs and that any potential Uyghur factions in Pakistan are firmly suppressed. As for Pakistan, it is beset with potential separatist movements such as those in Sindh and Balochistan (where Gwadar port is located). Even if the PLA does not directly involve itself in internal Pakistani affairs, the Chinese presence in Gwadar and elsewhere lends support to the government's efforts to maintain a unified Pakistan in the face of separatist factions in the provinces. The two governments' support for each other's right to act as they see fit in their domestic affairs and to sustain strong counter-insurgency efforts is consolidated by CPEC, in which – as will be demonstrated in subsequent chapters – the militaries of the two countries have a strong influence.

Thus, by critically deconstructing the established CPEC narrative and constructing a new narrative based on the four goals listed earlier – for which the chapters to come will present detailed evidence – the central aim of the book is to re-evaluate CPEC in order to ascertain exactly what it stands for and what it has – and has not – achieved in the first five years of its existence. In addition, the book is intended to draw out what it is realistic to expect from CPEC in the next ten years and beyond. It may be the case that CPEC serves to reinforce the idea that China's relationship with Pakistan is 'higher than the Himalayas, deeper than the ocean'. But at the same time, this book argues against the notion that the BRI's 'flagship project' is a 'game changer' and 'economic corridor' which will connect the two countries over the top of the earthquake-ridden, snowbound, geopolitically disputed Karakoram mountains. Instead, it posits that CPEC serves as a consolidation and expansion of the long-term China-Pakistan cooperation which predated the BRI. Although it contains the word 'economic' in its name, the China-Pakistan Economic Corridor is undoubtedly intended to support political and security goals as well as economic ones.

1.2 Deconstructing CPEC scholarship

Looking in detail at scholarly accounts of CPEC, one finds that certain aspects are over-emphasised while others are omitted. Most significantly, Pakistan's internal dynamics and problems tend to be under-emphasised in many analyses. Factors such as the inherent instability of the state, the domination of the nation's political and economic affairs by a Punjab-based civil-military elite, and strong separatist pressures emerging from regions such as Balochistan and Sindh have a bearing on the implementation and justification of CPEC which is not sufficiently acknowledged by many scholars publishing on CPEC. This is surprising given that such factors are well known to scholars of Pakistan's history, politics, society, and economic development (e.g. Siddiqa 2007; Nawaz 2008; Noman 2009). Above all, the conception of CPEC focuses on Chinese investments and infrastructure construction in Pakistan rather than across the border in China (or Afghanistan). Thus, the empirical reality of Pakistan's past and present circumstances needs to be incorporated into the analysis of what CPEC is and is not. Unlike much of the CPEC literature – such as it is – this book sets out to situate CPEC in Pakistan's circumstances – as well as in China and Pakistan's mostly complementary motivations for cooperation.

In marked contrast to the expectations of many observers, especially in Pakistan, CPEC cannot simply be seen as a 'game changer' for Pakistan: an injection of funds and construction which will magically transform this troubled nation into an economic powerhouse. This optimistic conception of CPEC, so prevalent in much of the discourse emerging from Pakistan, is as much misleading as it is utopian. The analysis contained in this book will demonstrate that there are many good reasons to believe that there are other drivers of CPEC beyond the 'game changer' narrative of economic transformation and regional integration. Most importantly, these include security and geopolitical considerations related to both China and Pakistan's border disputes with India and the suppression of separatist tendencies within each state.

For China, establishing a presence in Gwadar port is also likely to be motivated by its lack of an Indian Ocean port. For China, having a foothold on the Indian Ocean littoral gives it another long-term option in its quest to maintain the security of its maritime trade and energy supply routes – most notably from the nearby Persian Gulf. However, rather than building an oil pipeline from Gwadar, up through Pakistan, and over the Karakoram mountains into Xinjiang, China's goal, I argue, is to have a base from which it may, in the long term, be able to protect its national security interests in the Indian Ocean region (IOR). I call this *geopositional hedging*: establishing a position in a possibly strategic location – in this case near the Strait of Hormuz – in order to hedge against potential future risk. The US diplomat Henry Kissinger likens this element of Chinese strategy to a game of *weiqi* (usually called 'go' in the West) in which stones are placed on a board in order to encircle the opponent – or to prevent encirclement (Kissinger 2011: 23–25; see also Chapter 4).

In its examination of the scholarly literature on CPEC, this book takes a step beyond the standard literature review or state-of-the-art sections in many academic publications. Rather, what is intended here is a *deconstruction* of assumptions prevalent in the literature with the aim of *reconfiguring* how we understand CPEC. The aim is to present a rigorously empirical analysis of CPEC, so that researchers have an evidence-based foundation upon which to interrogate the aims and achievements of the megaproject instead of a set of recycled tropes – such as the prevalent one within Pakistan about CPEC being a 'game changer'.

Methodologically, the task of deconstruction and reconfiguration begins with a content analysis of 100 of the most-cited publications on CPEC: 60 in English and 40 in Chinese.[2] To analyse the texts, a combination of quantitative and qualitative content analysis was used. Quantitatively, a simple count of the number of publications which include terms such as 'game changer' and 'Malacca' was made to determine how many texts in the sample included these terms. Qualitatively, the texts were coded (i.e. categorised: see Elliott 2018: 2852) according to whether they included certain assumptions concerning CPEC. First and foremost, the texts in the sample were qualitatively analysed to evaluate whether they contained the assumption that there is a plan to construct an oil pipeline between Gwadar port in Pakistan and Xinjiang province in northwest China. A text was categorised as including the assumption that a pipeline was being planned from Gwadar to Xinjiang (1) if it mentioned a plan for such a pipeline in at least one sentence, and (2) if it did not critically interrogate that assumption anywhere in the text. The same process was conducted concerning other aspects of the texts: the results are included at salient points in the book. The methodological approach is essentially abductive (rather than purely deductive or inductive), in that the analysis feeds back into the re-evaluation of assumptions and theories about CPEC based on the empirical evidence examined in each chapter. Thus, the second step in the deconstruction and reconfiguration process involves evaluating the tropes and assumptions revealed in the content analysis by setting them against a range of empirical evidence concerning the real-world planning and implementation of the megaproject.

To illustrate the first step in the methodological approach used – and to begin the task of deconstruction and reconfiguration conducted abductively throughout the book – Table 1.1 reveals the prevalence of the 'game changer' trope in a representative sample of 60 scholarly publications on CPEC in English. Astoundingly, more than half of the publications included in the sample use the term. In addition, almost half (49%) of 100 publications in English and Chinese analysed mention the word 'Malacca'. Table 1.1 also reveals that out of 100 CPEC publications analysed in English and Chinese, 70 scholars assume – without rigorously interrogating the assumption – that a pipeline from Gwadar to Xinjiang is planned. Almost half of the publications (48%) also assume – again, without critical analysis – that such a pipeline is feasible.[3]

In this specific case, the second step in the abductive deconstruction and reconfiguration process involves evaluating the pipeline assumption according

Table 1.1 Prevalence of assumptions about CPEC in scholarly literature

	Phrase 'game changer' used	*'Malacca' mentioned*	*Assumes cross-border pipeline planned*	*Assumes cross-border pipeline feasible*
Publications in English (60)	58% (35)	55% (33)	73% (44)	62% (37)
Publications in Chinese (40)	N/A	40% (16)	65% (26)	27.5% (11)
All publications (100)	N/A	49% (49)	70% (70)	48% (48)

Source: author

to empirical evidence. As this book will demonstrate, according to officially published materials there is currently no plan on the table for such a pipeline (China-Pakistan Economic Corridor (CPEC) Official Website 2021). No concrete steps have been taken within Pakistan even to begin planning a Gwadar-Kashgar pipeline. It is also, as subsequent chapters will demonstrate, highly doubtful that such a pipeline is logistically feasible or economically viable. Yet, as Table 1.1 reveals, a large proportion of scholars assume – without interrogating the assumption in their text – that a Gwadar-Xinjiang pipeline is both planned and feasible. Thus, one of the major goals of this book is to deconstruct assumptions about CPEC – such as the 'Malacca dilemma' and 'game changer' tropes – and to generate a reconfigured understanding of the megaproject based on empirical evidence of its planning and implementation, as well as an evaluation of the Sino-Pakistani relationship – including each country's motivations for cooperation.

1.3 Generalisability

In discussing the problems inherent in the implementation of CPEC, the book also generates conclusions which reverberate beyond Pakistan. The BRI is an initiative which purportedly aims to connect Asia and Europe via a set of 'economic corridors'. Analysing the problems of CPEC in this regard allows one to draw out implications concerning the progress of the other parts of the BRI. Specifically, CPEC's problems – assumed goals not holding up under scrutiny, difficulties implementing investment and infrastructure projects, and lack of transparency – are to be found elsewhere along the route of China's New Silk Road, as the final chapter will demonstrate. The book's analysis can therefore provide food for thought for observers of BRI projects in other regions, as well as for those who study the impacts of the BRI at a broader level. It can also serve as a warning against taking established narratives concerning Chinese foreign policy at face value, no matter who is propagating them. The book provides a reminder that there is always a need, in the case of both China and other countries, to examine the received wisdom on any given policy initiative – foreign or domestic – and compare it to the empirical evidence of how a scheme is being implemented.

The methodology used in this book is to take the prevailing narratives about CPEC that have come to dominate debates on China-Pakistan relations and deconstruct them based on a range of empirical evidence: economic data, logistical considerations, security issues, and so on. Once deconstructed, the aim is to construct a new, evidentially based narrative with which to reconfigure understandings of the megaproject. Reconfiguring CPEC in this way is akin to looking at a jigsaw puzzle which has been put together wrong, including pieces taken from other puzzles. The task of the analyst is to disassemble the jigsaw puzzle, study the pieces carefully, and then try to connect them together in a more logical shape, discarding the pieces which do not belong. At the end, there may still be some gaps in the puzzle, some pieces missing; but the picture formed will have a clearer, more logical shape. This process of reconfiguration could be called discourse deconstruction/reconstruction – or disassembling and reassembling a puzzle. The name is not as important as the logic of the approach, which picks apart established tropes and narratives based on assumptions, half-baked ideas, public diplomacy, and wish-fulfilment, and replaces them with an evidence-based narrative. This is an approach which can be used to deconstruct and reconfigure established narratives concerning any large project involving two or more international actors.

In connection with the latter point, Chapter 2 focuses primarily on challenging the established narratives which unfortunately have been reproduced relatively uncritically in many scholarly publications about CPEC. The cumulative effect of these efforts is to endorse the received wisdom on CPEC passed down from official texts through the Pakistani and Chinese media and into international media, strongly influencing the global public's understanding of the megaproject. Although critiquing scholarly accounts is not the primary aim of the book – rather, it is to understand CPEC itself – Chapter 2's deconstruction of scholar-endorsed narratives, followed by a reconfiguration of how CPEC should instead be understood in Chapters 3–5, produces conclusions which can be applied to other international phenomena. The findings constitute a reminder that it behoves scholars to take pains to dig down beneath the surface of official narratives and media-dispersed tropes concerning policy initiatives – whoever is propagating them – and unearth an account which better represents the on-the-ground empirical reality.

1.4 Organisation and aims of the book

The book is organised as follows. Chapter 2 deconstructs the established narratives and tropes concerning CPEC, most notably those prevalent in scholarly texts. The chapter sets out to demonstrate that the historical record of China-Pakistan relations does not support the received wisdom of it as a transformative 'game changer', 'economic corridor', or as solving China's 'Malacca dilemma'. The chapter lays the foundation for constructing a new CPEC narrative based on empirical evidence which better represents the realities of the BRI's 'flagship project' and the motivations of the two partners, China and Pakistan. Chapter 3 then digs deeper into the 'game changer' and 'economic corridor' tropes by examining empirical evidence concerning Sino-Pakistani economic cooperation. The chapter shows that China's CPEC investments, while not insignificant, are not large enough to transform Pakistan's economy. It also casts doubt on the 'economic corridor' narrative of Pakistan as a hub for inter-regional integration between Central Asia, South Asia, and the Middle East. Chapter 4 takes the analysis a step further by examining the geographical, logistical, and geopolitical realities of connecting Pakistan with Xinjiang via the mountainous border region disputed with India. The analysis reveals that the construction of an oil pipeline to solve China's purported 'Malacca dilemma' is neither economically nor logistically viable. In fact, it is not even necessary given the fact that pipelines from Central Asia pass through Xinjiang, which itself has large oil and gas reserves (Chen 2020). There is also evidence to suggest that the Chinese have quietly shelved any notion of building a Pakistan-Xinjiang pipeline connection (Garlick 2018: 524–526). Chapter 5 moves from deconstruction to reconfiguration of the CPEC narrative by positing that the geopolitical and security aspects of the megaproject constitute its most important aspect. A range of empirical evidence for drawing this conclusion is outlined. Chapter 6 is the concluding chapter, wherein the findings of the book are summarised and dissected. Lessons are drawn from the analysis and comparison made with other 'economic corridor' projects under the umbrella of China's Belt and Road Initiative. CPEC's probable future trajectory is also outlined, and lessons concerning the interpretation of large-scale international cooperation projects are drawn out.

The book has five main aims. The first is to deconstruct the scholarly narrative of the China-Pakistan Economic Corridor, which is based on tropes recycled from official announcements. The second is to construct a new narrative based on the historical record of Sino-Pakistani cooperation, as well as the economic and political realities of CPEC's planning and implementation. The third is to reach some conclusions concerning long-term China-Pakistan cooperation which rest on empirical evidence rather than recycled tropes about the 'Malacca dilemma' and CPEC as a 'game changer'. The fourth is to understand the vagaries and limitations of China's involvement in developing countries it has included in the Belt and Road Initiative. And the fifth is to draw out some lessons about critiquing official and semi-official narratives on the planning and implementation of large-scale international investment projects – or any international cooperation initiatives. Overall, the main goal of the book in a generalisable sense is to demonstrate the need for critical interrogation of established narratives and tropes, especially those emanating from investment projects or other large-scale initiatives – no matter whether they originate from China or somewhere else.

Notes

1 There are too many publications to list here: see Chapter 2 for an analysis of recurring tropes in the scholarly literature on CPEC. See also Appendix 1 for a list of 100 publications on CPEC which were analysed as part of the research for this book.

2 The full list of publications included in the analysis is given in Appendix 1, which also outlines the methodology used to analyse the texts.

3 Interestingly, a far lower proportion (27.5%) of Chinese authors assume that a Gwadar-Xinjiang pipeline is feasible than authors writing in English (62%). Most of the authors publishing on CPEC are Pakistani scholars.

References

Ahmar, Moonis (2015) 'Strategic Meaning of the China-Pakistan Economic Corridor', *Strategic Studies*, Vol. 34/35, No. 4/1, pp. 35–49.

Alam, Khalid Mehmood, Xuemei Li, and Saranjam Baig (2019) 'Impact of Transport Cost and Travel Time on Trade Under China-Pakistan Economic Corridor (CPEC)', *Journal of Advanced Transportation*, Vol. 2019, Article ID 7178507: 1–16.

Bloomberg News (2021) 'How China's Flagship Belt and Road Project Stalled Out', 14 January. Available at: www.youtube.com/watch?v=AU1OvrbawE8&feature=youtu.be (accessed 25 May 2021).

Boni, Filippo (2020) *Sino-Pakistani Relations: Politics, Military and Regional Dynamics*, Abingdon, UK: Routledge.

Chen, Aizhu (2020) 'PetroChina Strikes Big Gas Find in China Xinjiang's Junggar Basin: State Media', *Reuters*, 21 December. Available at: www.reuters.com/article/us-china-gas-discovery-petrochina-idUSKBN28V084 (accessed 24 May 2021).

Cheng, Yunjie (2015) 'Research on Promoting China-Pakistan Trade Development Against the Background of the "China-Pakistan Economic Corridor"' (Zhōng bā jīngjì zǒuláng" bèijǐng xià tíshēng zhōng bā màoyì fāzhǎn wèntí yánjiū, 中巴经济走廊"背景下提升中巴贸易发展问题研究), *South Asian Studies Quarterly* (Nányà yánjiū jìkā, 南亚研究季刊), Vol. 2015, No. 2, pp. 94–101.

China-Pakistan Economic Corridor (CPEC) Official Website (2021) Available at: cpecinfo.com (accessed 20 May 2021).

Elliott, Victoria (2018) 'Thinking About the Coding Process in Qualitative Data Analysis', *The Qualitative Report*, Vol. 23, No. 11, pp. 2850–2861.

Garlick, Jeremy (2018) 'Deconstructing the China-Pakistan Economic Corridor: Pipe Dreams Versus Geopolitical Realities', *Journal of Contemporary China*, Vol. 27, No. 112, pp. 519–533.

Khan, Abdullah (2021) 'PIA: First Non-Communist Airline into China', *Global Village Space*, 11 May. Available at: www.globalvillagespace.com/pia-first-non-communist-airline-into-china/ (accessed 16 May 2021).

Kissinger, Henry (2011) *On China*, London: Allen Lane.

Lu, Shulin (2014/2015) 'China Pakistan Economic Corridor: A Flagship and Exemplary Project of "One Belt and One Road"', *Strategic Studies*, Vol. 34/35, No. 4/1, pp. 165–173.

Markey, Daniel S. (2020) *China's Western Horizon: Beijing and the New Geopolitics of Eurasia*, New York: Oxford University Press.

Nawaz, Shuja (2008) *Crossed Swords: Pakistan, Its Army, and the Wars Within*, Oxford: Oxford University Press.

Noman, Omar (2009) *Pakistan: Political and Economic History Since 1947*, Abingdon, UK: Routledge.

Reuters (2021) 'China Reveals Four Soldiers Killed in June 2020 Border Clash with India', 19 February. Available at: www.reuters.com/article/us-china-india-border-idUSKBN2AJ04B (accessed 25 May 2021).

Siddiqa, Ayesha (2007) *Military Inc.: Inside Pakistan's Military Economy*, London: Pluto Press.

Siddiqui, Salman (2017) 'CPEC Investment Pushed from $55b to $62b', *The Express Tribune*, 12 April. Available at: https://tribune.com.pk/story/1381733/cpec-investment-pushed-55b-62b/ (accessed 17 January 2021).

Yao, Yun (2015) 'The China-Pakistan Economic Corridor: A Risk Analysis' (Zhong ba jīngjì zǒuláng miànlín de fēngxiǎn fēnxi, 中巴经济走廊面临的风险分析), *South Asian Studies Quarterly* (Nányà yánjiū jìkān, 南亚研究季刊), Vol. 2015, No. 2, pp. 35–45.

Zhao, Jie, and Liu Ning (2017) 'The China-Pakistan Economic Corridor Connects to China: The Impact of Import and Export Trade' (Zhōng bā jīngjì zǒuláng guàntōng duì zhōngguó jìn chūkǒu màoyì de yǐngxiǎng, 中巴经济走廊贯通对中国进出口贸易的影响), *World Economic Research* (Shìjiè jīngjì yánjiū, 世界经济研究), Vol. 2017, No. 3, pp. 123–133.

2 Deconstructing established CPEC narratives

2.1 Introduction: of tropes and scholars

A great deal has been written about the China-Pakistan Economic Corridor since President Xi Jinping's visit to Pakistan in April 2015, when CPEC was semi-officially designated the 'flagship project' of Xi's Belt and Road Initiative (Lu 2014/2015: 170–171). However, as the examination of scholarly texts presented in this chapter will reveal, there has been a tendency for many observers to recycle official discourse and associated memes about CPEC uttered or rubber-stamped by leaders without adequate critical interrogation. The project's international image is shrouded in a mist of obfuscation resulting from the understandable tendency of Chinese and Pakistani scholars and observers to stick to the officially endorsed version of aims and progress. As a result, recycled phrases devoid of meaningful content such as 'win-win' outcomes and the project being designated a 'game changer' have tended to proliferate in much of the CPEC literature (e.g. Abid and Ashfaq 2015: 159; Afzal and Naseem 2018: 213; Malik 2018).

Although not ideal, the recycling of tropes and phrases in the media without adequate critique might be expected due to tight deadlines, decreasing funds, and lack of time for journalists to carry out in-depth research (although it must be noted that, in fact, there is a surprising amount of critical coverage of CPEC and other news stories in Pakistan by outlets such as *Dawn* and *Business Recorder*, thus casting doubt on the idea that Pakistani media cannot provide critical perspectives on official narratives). However, it is scholars rather than journalists who are under examination here. If recycled tropes were found to be prevalent in the scholarly literature that would be a matter of grave concern. One would expect scholars – who are generally held to a far higher standard of rigour than journalists, given their lengthy academic training – to challenge the received wisdom on an issue by interrogating it and verifying or negating it according to an evidential record. If this does not happen, and instead well-worn official phrases are repeated in the scholarly literature, a stamp of veracity is given to unexamined tropes. Eventually these tropes filter into the public sphere via media reports, in which the views of scholars, obtained via interviews, are often cited as supporting evidence. If recycled in this way, tropes become familiar and even accepted through constant repetition.

DOI: 10.4324/9781003018377-2

For this reason, this chapter critically examines a representative section of the scholarly literature on CPEC in English and Chinese to ascertain just how prevalent are the tropes of 'Malacca dilemma' and game changer', as well as the supposed plan for a cross-border oil pipeline. CPEC is generally seen as an infrastructure megaproject whose core focus is a goods transportation corridor between Pakistan and China, including, according to many accounts, a pipeline. In the scholarly literature, I posit, the hypothetical pipeline has itself become a trope which is repeated without sufficient interrogation. In fact, according to the official CPEC website's list of projects, no pipeline has yet even been planned, let alone built (CPEC 2021).

This chapter thus investigates whether scholars assume such tropes to be valid or challenge them by examining their relation to the real-world implementation of CPEC. It is an attempt, above all, to identify and elucidate CPEC memes and tropes and to separate them from the reality of the project in order to assess its on-the-ground implementation and impacts in subsequent chapters. Accordingly, the chapter is based on a content analysis of 100 publications, 60 in English and 40 in Chinese, to determine the extent to which well-worn phrases such as 'game changer' and 'Malacca dilemma' fill the work of CPEC scholars. The texts are also analysed quantitatively to ascertain how many of them assume that the construction of a cross-border oil pipeline is planned and feasible.

The first section examines the 'economic corridor' concept to obtain a working definition and then assess the extent to which the concept matches the reality of CPEC. The second section attempts to separate the official discourse and scholarly interpretations concerning the 'Malacca dilemma' trope from the on-the-ground implementation of the megaproject that has occurred. The third section digs down beneath the surface of the project and extracts the underlying motivations for cooperation on both sides based on the history of the partnership, challenging the 'game changer' trope. The fourth section examines the historical record of China-Pakistan cooperation: the aim is to challenge the 'game changer' trope by establishing that CPEC is essentially a continuation – albeit admittedly an intensifying – of already-established cooperation. The final section draws out the lessons to be learnt from the analysis regarding the planning and execution of international megaprojects involving cooperation between two or more countries.

2.2 To what extent is CPEC really an 'economic corridor'?

One might assume, as many authors do (e.g. Zhang 2014), that an 'economic corridor' ought to be primarily concerned with goods movement and the construction of infrastructure such as ports, roads, railways, and power plants along the route. However, in the case of CPEC such an assumption should not be taken at face value. As analysis throughout this chapter will demonstrate, CPEC has political and military aspects which undermine its standard conception as an investment-driven infrastructure megaproject under the umbrella of the BRI. At the very minimum, the 'economic corridor' concept is a contested one which lacks clarity in both the literature and the implementation of CPEC. As will be revealed in this and the next chapter, it is not even clear that cross-border trade (incorporating regional integration) is the main aim or achievement of CPEC. If cross-border trade is not the central focus of the megaproject, this inherently undermines the idea of an 'economic corridor' in any meaningful sense. Thus, while CPEC certainly contains elements of an infrastructure megaproject, classifying it as primarily an 'economic corridor' is problematic.

Scholarly attempts to clarify the 'economic corridor' concept have produced varied and not always satisfactory results. In the case of CPEC, the most notable attempt at a definition is that of Wolf (2020: 21–46). However, Wolf's extended ruminations lack overall clarity because his framework contains no fewer than 18 'key indicators' of economic corridors (Wolf 2020: 45–46). With greater concision, Brunner (2013: 1) posits that "economic corridors connect economic agents along a defined geography" but that they "are not mere transport connections along which people and goods move." He suggests that "they have to be analyzed as part of integrated economic networks, such as global and regional value chains and production networks" (Brunner 2013: 1). If one uses Brunner's definition, CPEC would presumably need to not only provide a transport connection between Pakistan and China but also be steadily integrated into regional and global value chains via the Chinese-controlled port of Gwadar and other connectivity-related infrastructure.

At the time of its formal announcement, in April 2015, it seemed that CPEC was intended to be what it says on the tin: a connectivity corridor enhancing the economies of the two partners by transforming the logistics of cross-border and intraregional trade. US$46 billion of investment in infrastructure and energy projects was promised (Yao 2015: 36) – a sum which increased two years later to US$62 billion (Siddiqui 2017). In November 2015, the port of Gwadar, situated on the Indian Ocean littoral not far from the Strait of Hormuz and the oil producing Gulf states, was leased for 40 years to the Chinese Overseas Ports Holding Company (Panda 2015). From there, a transport corridor was supposed to snake its way up to the northern border and cross into China's northwestern Xinjiang province. In addition to the existing road, plans for oil pipelines and railway connections were reported (Liu 2015: 99–100). These were supposed to solve China's 'Malacca dilemma' – the idea that China's reliance on sea routes constitutes a security risk – by connecting the Chinese mainland to the Indian Ocean by a direct overland route.

However, as Chapter 4 will demonstrate, there are many reasons – and copious evidence – to believe that CPEC is not solely – or even primarily – intended to generate cross-border goods transportation. Numerous physical obstacles and security considerations weigh heavily on the implementation of the megaproject. Most notably, it should be remembered that border conflicts and geopolitical rivalry with neighbouring India loom large in the calculations of both Chinese and Pakistani planners. Furthermore, in addition to being disputed with India, the border area through which CPEC's Karakoram Highway passes en route from

Gwadar to Kashgar is mountainous and difficult to access. The region is prone to severe earthquakes since it lies on a fault line where the Indian and Eurasian tectonic plates collide. One earthquake in 2010 caused landslides which created a lake which submerged a section of the Karakoram Highway, necessitating the construction of tunnels and bridges to bypass the lake, a process which took five years (Garlick 2018: 524; see also Chapter 4). The Highway, constructed in the 1970s, remains the only overland connection between China and Pakistan. The Khunjerab Pass, where the Karakoram Highway crosses from Gilgit-Baltistan into Xinjiang at a height of 4693 metres above sea level, is impassable for several months in winter due to heavy snow (Wolf 2020: 123).

The obstacles to the implementation of CPEC as a cross-border connectivity project do not end with the condition of the Karakoram Highway. A fibre-optic cable connection, the first phase of which already connects Khunjerab with Rawalpindi (Bhutta 2020), *is* in the process of being laid between Xinjiang and Gwadar. However, there is at the time of writing no evidence of the planning or commencement of railway or pipeline construction projects over the Karakoram mountains (China-Pakistan Economic Corridor (CPEC) Official Website 2021). There is no official explanation of why cross-border railway and pipeline projects are not included in the official list, but their absence provides clear evidence that there is no plan to build them anytime soon. Another issue arises from the poor security environment within Pakistan. Separatist movements – such as the Balochistan independence movement – affect the security of trans-Pakistan transport and energy infrastructure. This is one of the reasons why, throughout the process of implementing CPEC, the Pakistani army has played a leading role in the security, organisation, and even construction of its constituent projects (Wolf 2016; Boni 2020). A further problem is with the slow rate of progress on the construction of Gwadar port. The development of Gwadar – located in separatist Balochistan – is shrouded in mystery due to a lack of transparency and access to foreign journalists. Be this as it may, there is reason to believe that construction of the port has been much slower than expected and that the volumes of cargo being offloaded there are relatively insignificant (see Chapter 3).

Furthermore, observers who believe that CPEC is purely an infrastructure construction project designed to solve China's 'Malacca dilemma', enhance mutual trade, and connect Pakistan and Xinjiang to global value chains need to complexify their outlook by studying the intersection of political, military, and economic factors in the calculations of Chinese and Pakistani leaders. The idea of CPEC as an 'economic corridor' – an idea which is embedded in the name of the megaproject and thus generally assumed to be true – should not necessarily be taken at face value. If it can be shown that the main achievement of CPEC so far has been to develop infrastructure within Pakistan rather than across the border, then the idea of Pakistan being used as an 'economic corridor' connecting the Indian Ocean with Xinjiang and Central Asia becomes inherently questionable due to the lack of progress on cross-border connectivity. The remainder of this chapter – and the whole book – aims to challenge the predominant 'economic corridor' CPEC narrative via the following methods: (1) deconstruction of the officially endorsed discourse recycled by many scholars, (2) examination of the historical record of Sino-Pakistani cooperation and the long-term motivations of the partners for pursuing and consolidating their partnership, and (3) analysis of a wide range of empirical evidence concerning the planning and implementation of CPEC in the context of Pakistan and China's security and the geopolitics of the Indian Ocean and South Asian regions. In the remainder of this chapter, the analysis proceeds with an examination of the 'Malacca dilemma' and 'game changer' tropes.

2.3 'Malacca dilemma': discourse versus reality

Discussion of the 'Malacca dilemma' originates in a speech by Hu Jintao in 2003, where he discussed China's vulnerability to blockade of its oil imports from the Middle East (Lanteigne 2008: 144). However, the idea for Chinese development of Gwadar port and the construction of oil and gas pipelines from there to Kashgar in China's northwestern Xinjiang province was reportedly initiated by former Pakistani President Pervez Musharraf (Lu 2014/2015: 165; Markey 2020: vii; Boni 2020: 82). Putting the two presidents' ideas together eventually gave rise to what came to be commonly perceived as the rationale for CPEC from China's supposed point of view: an overland corridor for transporting oil and other goods from the Indian Ocean to China, as well as in the reverse direction. This perception generally includes the assumption that a key goal of CPEC, as far as China is concerned, is to construct a pipeline to transport oil (delivered by tankers) from Gwadar over the Himalayas to Kashgar and beyond. However, a pipeline project was not included in the list of 51 memoranda of understanding (MoUs) published upon the official announcement of CPEC in April 2015 (The Nation 2015). The only pipeline project listed on the official CPEC website as of May 2021 was an incomplete liquid national gas pipeline between Gwadar and Nawabshah in Sindh province to the east (CPEC 2021). No oil pipeline was mentioned anywhere in official sources. Nor was there any mention of cross-border pipeline projects. The absence of official mention of trans-Himalayan pipeline projects casts doubt on the notion that transporting oil from Gwadar to Xinjiang is a core element of CPEC.

Close analysis of 60 of the most heavily cited (by 2020) scholarly publications in English on CPEC reveals that the assumption that a Gwadar-Xinjiang oil pipeline was planned (an idea which is connected to the 'Malacca dilemma' trope) occurs in 44 (73%) of them (see Table 2.1). When a statement concerning the possibility of a cross-border pipeline was discovered in the texts, a search was conducted for evidence of critical interrogation of the assumption. Where there was no such critique – not even in one sentence – the publication was designated as assuming the item to be true. Texts were further examined, using the same method, to ascertain whether authors assumed that building and maintaining such a pipeline would be (1) feasible, (2) economically sustainable, and (3) secure.

Using this approach, the finding was that 25 out of 30 publications (83%) on CPEC published in the period 2015–2017 assumed that a trans-Himalayan

Table 2.1 Assumptions about cross-border pipeline in English-language scholarly literature

	Assumes cross-border pipeline is planned	*Assumes cross-border pipeline is feasible*	*Assumes cross-border pipeline will be economically sustainable*	*Assumes cross-border pipeline will be secure*
Publications 2015–2017 (30)	83% (25)	70% (21)	47% (14)	7% (2)
Publications 2018–2020 (30)	63% (19)	53% (16)	27% (8)	7% (2)
Publications 2015–2020 (60)	73% (44)	62% (37)	37% (22)	7% (4)

Source: author

pipeline was planned without critically interrogating the assumption. Out of 30 publications (70%) published in the same period, 21 assumed that constructing such a pipeline was feasible. In the period 2018–2020 the numbers dropped somewhat to 63 per cent and 53 per cent, respectively, but this still means that over half of the scholars who wrote on the topic of CPEC three to four years after it began assumed that a pipeline was both planned and feasible without any attempt to examine empirical evidence from the intervening period. On the other hand, fewer than half of the authors – 47 per cent in the earlier period and 27 per cent in the later one – assumed uncritically that such a pipeline would be economically sustainable. Curiously, fewer still – 7 per cent in each period – assumed that the pipeline would be secure. This means that most commentators understood the economic and security risks at least to some extent but still assumed that a cross-border pipeline was both planned and feasible. The findings reveal a curious mixture of assumptions concerning the hypothetical pipeline – which is not mentioned among the projects listed on the official CPEC website (CPEC 2021). Most authors recognised both that the economical sustainability of the pipeline was in question and that it would be difficult to maintain the security of the pipeline. Despite acknowledging these problems, they persisted in assuming that such a pipeline was both planned and feasible without any sign of critical interrogation of those assumptions.

Among Chinese scholars, a somewhat lower level of confidence in the planning, feasibility, economic sustainability, and security of a hypothetical Gwadar-Xinjiang pipeline is evident (see Table 2.2). Approximately two-thirds (65%) of scholars assume that a cross-border pipeline is planned, which is only slightly lower than the figure for scholars publishing in the English language. On the other hand, there is a markedly lower level of confidence in the feasibility and economic sustainability of the hypothetical pipeline than among English-language authors.

Table 2.2 Assumptions about cross-border pipeline in Chinese-language scholarly literature

	Assumes cross-border pipeline is planned	*Assumes cross-border pipeline is feasible*	*Assumes cross-border pipeline will be economically sustainable*	*Assumes cross-border pipeline will be secure*
Publications 2013–2016 (20)	75% (15)	30% (6)	30% (6)	10% (2)
Publications 2017–2019 (20)	55% (11)	25% (5)	20% (4)	0% (0)
Publications 2013–2019 (40)	65% (26)	27.5% (11)	25% (10)	5% (2)

Source: author

As with the English-language group, few scholars (2 out of 40) assume that the hypothetical pipeline would be secure once constructed.

Overall, the analysis of 100 articles in English and Chinese reveals that 70 per cent of scholars assume that a pipeline from Gwadar to Xinjiang is definitely planned. Almost half (48%) of the authors assume that the construction of such a pipeline is feasible without critically interrogating the assumption with reference to the logistics of construction and the terrain through which the pipeline would have to pass. Approximately one-third (32%) of the scholars assume that the hypothetical pipeline would be economically sustainable. The area in which scholars are most willing to engage in critical analysis is with regard to the security of the pipeline: very few (6%) assume that it will be secure. Many authors point out threats to the security of such a pipeline. It is strange, therefore, that some of these scholars do not appear to link security threats to questions of economic sustainability or feasibility.

In fact, there is copious evidence to suggest that constructing a trans-Himalayan pipeline connecting Pakistan and China would be a very difficult and expensive enterprise. Apart from the high financial cost of construction and maintenance (for details of which see the following paragraph), other serious obstacles include the following: the fact that the border zone lies on a tectonic fault line; the extremely challenging mountainous terrain, the probability of attempts by separatists/terrorists to disrupt the flow of oil, and the reality that the border area connecting Pakistan and China is disputed with India (Garlick 2018). Many of the same issues would also affect any attempt to construct and maintain other transport infrastructure such as a trans-Himalayan railway.

Regarding cost, Erickson and Collins (2010: 102–103) point out that any pipeline would need an expensive and energy-intensive system for pumping oil up to a height of 4500 metres. Mei Xinyu, a research fellow at the Chinese Academy

Table 2.3 Assumptions about cross-border pipeline in scholarly literature

	Assumes cross-border pipeline is planned	*Assumes cross-border pipeline is feasible*	*Assumes cross-border pipeline will be economically sustainable*	*Assumes cross-border pipeline will be secure*
English-language publications (60)	73% (44)	62% (37)	37% (22)	7% (4)
Chinese-language publications (40)	65% (26)	27.5% (11)	25% (10)	5% (2)
Total publications (100)	70% (70)	48% (48)	32% (32)	6% (6)

Source: author

of International Trade and Economic Cooperation under the Ministry of Commerce, notes that a pipeline would also pass through terrain frozen in winter, necessitating the use of a heating system to ensure that oil would not freeze in the pipe (Li 2016). Given the costs of installing such systems, a trans-Himalayan pipeline would not be able to compete with the relatively low cost of transporting oil by sea to China's east coast, where most of China's industrial centres are located (Erickson and Collins 2010: 104).

Another connected point is that there are already oil and gas pipelines from Kazakhstan and Turkmenistan passing through Xinjiang. Xinjiang has its own oil fields, including recent additional discoveries: drilling for further reserves is ongoing (Chen 2020). The sparsely populated region therefore already has plenty of oil which needs to be pumped eastwards to China's industrial centres on the Pacific coast. These factors, allied to the relative cheapness of the maritime transportation route, imply that pumping oil over the Karakoram mountains from Pakistan into Xinjiang is not necessary, logical, or cost-effective. Indeed, an expert called Mei affiliated with the Chinese government concludes in an article in the state-endorsed Chinese newspaper *Global Times* entitled 'Gwadar Port benefits to China limited' that it makes more sense to invest in super-sized crude tankers than a trans-Himalayan connection (Li 2016). The same article also cites the Chinese shipping analyst Wu Minghua casting doubt on the cost-effectiveness of offloading oil from tankers at Gwadar and transporting the fuel by pipeline to China. Wu notes the low capacity of the port in comparison to China's overall oil demand, implying that "Gwadar will not become China's main trade hub with Persian Gulf countries, not to mention serve as an alternative route to the Malacca Straits" (Li 2016). Thus, there is evidence that the Chinese realised that the cost and difficulty of constructing and running a cross-border pipeline would be economically unsustainable and quietly dropped the idea without any official fanfare as long ago as 2016.

In fact, as already stated, no pipeline construction project across the Karakoram mountains is included in the list of energy projects on the official CPEC website (see Table 2.4). None of the energy projects even involve connections between China and Pakistan or any activity on Chinese soil. Instead, all the projects listed are energy infrastructure projects within Pakistan and are intended to enhance Pakistan's chronically poor energy sector. All are therefore concerned with the production of energy via the construction and development of power plants

Table 2.4 CPEC energy infrastructure projects

Project	*Construction timeline*
2 × 660MW Coal-fired Power Plants at Port Qasim Karachi	2015–2018
Suki Kinari Hydropower Station, Naran, Khyber Pukhtunkhwa	2016–2022
Sahiwal 2x660MW Coal-fired Power Plant, Punjab	2015–2017
Engro Thar Block II 2 × 330MW Coal-fired Power Plant and Surface mine in block II of Thar Coal field, 3.8 million tonnes/year	2016–2019
Hydro China Dawood Wind Farm (Gharo, Thatta)	2015–2017
300MW Imported Coal Based Power Project at Gwadar	2017–unknown
Quaid-e-Azam 1000MW Solar Park (Bahawalpur)	2016
UEP Wind Farm (Jhimpir, Thatta)	2015–2017
Sachal Wind Farm (Jhimpir, Thatta)	2015–2017
SSRL Thar Coal Block-I 6.8 mtpa & SEC Mine Mouth Power Plant (2 × 660MW)	2017–2023
HUBCO Thar Coal Power Project (Thar Energy)	2021
ThalNova Thar Coal Power Project	2021
Karot Hydropower Station	2015–2021
Three Gorges Second & Third Wind Power Project	2016–2018
CPHGC 1,320MW Coal-fired Power Plant, Hub	2017–2019
Matiari to Lahore 660kV HVDC Transmission Line Project and Matiari (Port Qasim) – Faisalabad Transmission Line Project	2016–2021
Thar Mine Mouth Oracle Power Plant (1320MW) & surface mine	Unknown
Kohala Hydel Project, AJK	2018–2026
Cacho 50MW Wind Power Project	Unknown
Western Energy (Pvt.) Ltd. 50 MW Wind Power Project	Unknown
Azad Pattan Hydel Project, AJK	2026
Phandar Hydropower Station	Unknown
Gilgit KIU Hydropower	Unknown

Source: CPEC official website, at http://cpec.gov.pk/energy (accessed 6 March 2021)

and mines. The other notable focus of CPEC projects is on transport infrastructure within Pakistan. The only new cross-border physical infrastructure project mentioned on the official CPEC website, out of 73 projects listed, is a fibre-optic cable (CPEC 2021). This was included among the April 2015 MoUs (The Nation 2015). It has been completed and connects Khunjerab with Rawalpindi. With this single exception, Chinese investments thus far have been overwhelmingly concerned with constructing energy and transportation infrastructure within Pakistan rather than generating international connectivity or enhancing Pakistan's role in global value chains.

To understand why CPEC takes the form outlined here and is depicted as the BRI's 'flagship project' in South Asia despite its lack of progress in terms of overland connectivity infrastructure, it is necessary to examine the history of China-Pakistani relations and each side's motivations for engagement. If it can be demonstrated that CPEC is essentially a continuation of the historical cooperation initiated in the 1960s, then the megaproject may be seen as a consolidation and entrenchment of Sino-Pakistani cooperation rather than an economic 'game changer'. The next two sections consist of an analysis of scholarly discourse concerning the 'game changer' trope and a historical analysis of the factors and motivations involved in China's cooperation with Pakistan over the decades since the Sino-Indian War of 1962. Taken together, these analyses challenge the economics-based 'game changer' trope.

2.4 'Game changer'? What 'game changer'?

As noted in Chapter 1, the notion of CPEC as a 'game changer' appears to have been introduced into the official, semi-official, media, and scholarly discourse on the megaproject by Pakistani Prime Minister Nawaz Sharif during the megaproject's launch (Ahmar 2015: 48). One would expect that scholars would thereafter take on the responsibility of critically examining the notion of CPEC as a 'game changer', especially given the metaphorical nature of the slogan. One would imagine they would attempt to draw out some conclusions about exactly which 'game' is supposed to be in the process of being 'changed' through rigorous analysis of the evidence. However, unfortunately there has generally been a lack of critical engagement with the 'game changer' metaphor amid a tendency to recycle it without critical interrogation. An examination of the scholarly literature reveals that it has even failed to clarify precisely what developments the expression is referencing. This is not surprising given that in the study of international relations (IR), as Michael Marks points out, "metaphors used casually often are not investigated with regard to their validity for giving insight into the subject matter at hand" (Marks 2011: 5).

Still, it is remarkable how many scholars – especially those based in Pakistan – have employed the 'game changer' metaphor as an overriding – but vague – explanation of CPEC's purported benefits containing various levels of critically uninterrogated speculation and poorly supported prediction. For instance,

Ahmad et al (2017: 27) claim that CPEC is "a game changer which could help to incorporate and bond together the Central Asia, South Asia, and the Middle East economies." Abid and Ashfaq (2015: 142) suggest that CPEC "is a game changer project which will transform the fate of Pakistan and will help Pakistan modernize." According to them, it is also "a game-changer in the whole region by generating massive trade and economic activity" and "a game changer [which] will make China a real stakeholder in Pakistan's stability and security" (Abid and Ashfaq 2015: 159). Hussain (2017: 7) states that CPEC is "a game-changer for the country's economic development and security, as well as for the larger neighborhood." Chaziza (2016: 1) describes CPEC as "a game-changer for the Middle East", as well as a "long-awaited game-changer helping Beijing to expand its influence in the region" (Chaziza 2016: 6). He also claims that "Gwadar port may well ultimately be a strategic game changer" (Chaziza 2016: 8). Afzal and Naseem (2018: 210) designate CPEC "a game changer for the whole region" without explaining to which region they are referring. Expanding on the 'game changer' trope, they go so far as to label CPEC "this El-Dorado" (Afzal and Naseem 2018: 209). Makhdoom et al (2018: 45) designate CPEC "a game changer project for Pakistan", with a list of purported potential benefits that CPEC "will" bring, including "new avenues for business and trade in Pakistan", "enhance[d] geo-political importance of Pakistan", and "build[ing] positive image of Pakistan at global level."

Thus, CPEC's 'game changer' narrative appears to mean whatever the observer wants it to mean. In the use of the term, critical distance is generally lacking, and it is often not clear exactly which 'game' scholars believe is being 'changed' by CPEC. One might assume that the principal 'game' being 'changed' would be the transformation of Pakistan's dire economic circumstances by coordinated Chinese investment. However, as the previous paragraph demonstrates, scholars have mingled many other elements into the 'game changer' trope. These elements include enhanced regional integration, security issues, the development of Gwadar port, drawing China deeper into cooperation with Pakistan, and even an enhanced global status for Pakistan.

It is therefore necessary to conduct an examination of the historical record surrounding Sino-Pakistani cooperation since the 1960s to reveal each side's core motivations for sustaining cooperation. Understanding these motivations raises questions about the importance of the economic 'game changer' narrative with reference to the planning and implementation of CPEC. Instead, by considering a range of evidence derived from the historical record of cooperation, the 'game changer' trope can be replaced by a maintenance/consolidation narrative of deeper Sino-Pakistani cooperation, primarily in the areas of security and geopolitics. The reconfigured narrative thereby established relates primarily to the long-term security goals of both partners and the mitigation of the serious problems inherent in Pakistan's economy rather than an ambitious goal of somehow transforming Pakistan into the hub of a vast and interconnected Central Asia-South Asia-Middle East economic zone.

2.5 The historical record: challenging the 'game changer' narrative

Pakistan's entrenched enmity with its neighbour India, from which it separated amid bitter Hindu-Muslim violence in 1947, dominates the nation's calculations concerning cooperation with China. Since its foundation, Pakistan has also been perpetually short of foreign exchange reserves and in urgent need of large-scale investment to improve its energy and transport sectors. However, instability due to separatist attacks and other political uncertainties have made it historically difficult to identify foreign actors willing to take the risk of investing in Pakistan. From the Chinese perspective, geopolitical rivalry and border conflicts with India tend to be the main drivers of China's engagement with Pakistan. In addition, the fact that Pakistan, even if ostensibly possessing democratic institutions, is de facto controlled by a combination of civilian and military elites informs many aspects of the nation's close relations with China.

Studying Pakistan's history since its separation from India and foundation in 1947 reveals that the country is an inherently unstable entity formed out of the forced union of culturally distinct ethnic groups (Nawaz 2008: xxvii). Although almost all Pakistanis are Muslims, Pakistan is not so much a nation with a unified identity as a loose cluster of distinct ethnicities held together by the state's well-funded military. Elites from the most powerful province – Punjab – dominate the army and civilian power structures, forming a "military-bureaucratic complex" (Noman 2009: 12). Thus, the Chinese government knows that to gain influence in Pakistan, it must engage with the elite group which de facto runs the country.

Since Bangladesh (formerly East Pakistan) fought and won its independence in a bitter civil war in 1971 (in which India decisively intervened), Pakistan has consisted of four provinces. These are Punjab, Sindh, Balochistan, and Khyber Pakhtunkhwa. The capital city Islamabad is federally administered as the Islamabad Capital Territory. There are also two administrative territories which have not received full provincial status: Gilgit-Baltistan, and Azad Jammu and Kashmir. Of these administrative units, Punjab has by far the largest population, around 110 million out of a total of 212 million. The most privileged Punjabis and the descendants of Muslims who fled India after the partition constitute what Noman (2009: 8) calls a "tiny mahajjir-Punjabi élite". This educated urban class living in the cities of Islamabad, Lahore, and Karachi dominates the government and military. The predominance of this class in the elite structures of governance leads to resentment among outsider groups such as the Balochis and Sindhs because of perceived disenfranchisement. These groups are largely excluded from political decision-making, as well as having limited or no access to education (Pakistan has a high rate of illiteracy) and the economic advantages that the urban elites enjoy. Pakistan's problems with separatism and terrorist activity – which affect the security and implementation of CPEC – are thus explicable with reference to its history of domination of the nation's political economy by urban elites mainly based in Punjab.

Shah (2014: 1) and Nawaz (2008: xxviii) point out that the army has tended to exert control over the political life of Pakistan for almost all of its relatively brief existence. Historically, from the 1950s onwards, democratically elected governments have on several occasions been removed from power by the military when their decisions run counter to the interests of the elite. The historical record makes clear who is "effectively in control of Pakistan's political system, behind the façade of parliamentary institutions" (Noman 2009: 11). The Chief of Army Staff thereby becomes the most powerful man in the country, even if he does not make many public appearances. The military also dominates the economy (Siddiqa 2007). From partition onwards, more government funds have been allocated to the army than to development, resulting in rural impoverishment (Noman 2009: 19). The high allocation of resources to the military has restricted Pakistan's economic growth and generated a self-inflicted debt trap on the country, which therefore is perpetually short of foreign exchange reserves. Given the high level of influence the military has in Pakistan, it should come as no surprise that the first head of the CPEC Authority created in November 2019 was a retired lieutenant general called Asim Bajwa, who also served as a special assistant to Prime Minister Imran Khan.

The friendship between China and Pakistan stems from the time of China's brief 1962 border war with India, which China won, humiliating India. From that time forward, territorial disputes with India have constituted the foundation of the Sino-Pakistani 'all weather' alliance, persuading the two partners that their best course is to cooperate in the face of a common enemy. Surprisingly, Pakistan generally lacks close allies in the Muslim world and senses that US support is fickle. Islamabad, as Prime Minister Imran Khan discovered within a year of taking office in 2018, is thus forced to seek material and ideational support from China. The Chinese government has also struggled to attract reliable allies with sufficient heft to impact the regional balance of power, so the partnership with Pakistan has historically been important for Beijing in forming a wedge against India. The alliance also gives China a strategic foothold on the Indian Ocean via the port of Gwadar, enabling Beijing to push back somewhat against US military power in the Indian Ocean region.

Even though China stopped short of intervening on Pakistan's side in its conflicts with India in 1965 and 1971, it has assisted in Pakistan's development of military technology. Pakistan has been unable to obtain arms from Russia since Moscow has "entrenched defense ties with India" (Lam 2015: 226). Indeed, to both Islamabad and Beijing's dismay, Russia is the largest supplier of arms to India, Moscow's 'traditional ally': from 2004 to 2016 Russia sold US$25.2 billion of weapons to India, "dwarfing China's $5.2 billion sales to Pakistan in the same period and US sales to India" (Jackson 2018: 258). China has been vital to the Pakistan army's defence effort over the long term as Pakistan's largest supplier, having maintained a 47 per cent share of the Pakistani arms market between 2004 and 2015 (Jackson 2018: 261). At the same time as finding business for its weapons manufacturers, China has also been motivated to assist Pakistan by its need to counter the Russian-supplied Indian military build-up. By the 1990s, military technology cooperation with China had enabled Pakistan to acquire nuclear weapons as a counter to India's, even though the Chinese deny that they directly assisted in the development of such weapons (Boni 2020: 40). Leaders in the Chinese PLA therefore have a higher degree of influence than usual in China's policy towards Pakistan due to the long-term cooperation between the two countries' militaries (Lam 2015: 229).

Thus, the geopolitics and security aspects of the India issue must not be underestimated in assessing the rationale for CPEC, even if the megaproject is generally depicted by Beijing and Islamabad purely as a form of transformative economic cooperation. From the Chinese perspective, investing in Pakistan is fraught with risks due to security issues and the high probability of losing invested capital. China continues to support Pakistan because the partners' security interests coincide in two main areas. First, both wish to suppress separatism and therefore cooperate on counter-terrorism measures and intelligence. For China it is vital to combat insurgency in Xinjiang and it needs to ensure that support for the Uyghurs does not come across the border from Pakistan. Second, the alliance with Pakistan strengthens China's hand in its border disputes with India.

Issues related to geopolitics and security are especially pertinent to the Chinese-run port of Gwadar. Most importantly, it remains unclear what exactly the Chinese intend to do with the port. Gwadar was previously an Omani enclave which was sold to Pakistan in 1958 for US$3 million (Anwar 2010: 98). It remained largely undeveloped by Pakistan until the Chinese agreed to construct a commercial port in 2001. The first phase of construction was completed in 2007, and the port was opened to limited maritime traffic. However, although Gwadar has been called a deep seaport, the approach to the harbour is relatively shallow, meaning that further dredging is necessary if the port is to be able to accommodate larger vessels such as oil tankers (Garlick 2018: 525). Consequently, a second phase of development was planned. However, this second phase is still apparently in progress at the time of writing. Details of progress on the development of Gwadar are hard to find due to a lack of transparency surrounding the development of the port.

As already noted, Gwadar was leased to the Chinese company China Overseas Ports Holding Company (COPHC) in 2015 on a 40-year contract. This gives the Chinese licence to develop the port as a Chinese enclave – potentially serving as an Indian Ocean stronghold – without having to accommodate the demands of Balochis in the area. The development of Gwadar is viewed by both Beijing and Islamabad as a key part of CPEC. The official CPEC website (CPEC 2021) reveals that in addition to the dredging of the port, transport infrastructure, including an airport and highways, is being constructed. Work is also underway on a school, a hospital, and a wastewater plant as part of the Gwadar Smart Port City Master Plan.

Rumours abound that China intends to use Gwadar for military purposes. However, as yet there is no evidence that the port is being developed for use by the People's Liberation Army Navy (PLAN) (Iwanek 2019). Chinese military vessels do not appear to have visited the port. Nevertheless, the Chinese acquisition of its first overseas naval base in the East African nation of Djibouti in 2017 demonstrates China's expanding military interests in the Indian Ocean region (Blanchard 2017). In 2011, a PLA general admitted China's long-term intent to acquire foreign ports for military use (Lam 2015: 232). The Chinese development of other Indian Ocean ports such as Hambantota in Sri Lanka and Kyaukpyu in Myanmar worries the United States and India because – along with Gwadar – it is alleged to be an attempt to create a network of maritime military and commercial facilities along Chinese sea lines of communication (SLOCs). This collection of ports was dubbed China's "string of pearls" in an internal report supplied by the defence contractor Booz Allen Hamilton to the US defense department in 2004 (Washington Times 2005). Suggestively, a retired Pakistani naval officer in 2017 claimed that Gwadar.

> will allow the Chinese Navy to establish a robust foothold in the Indian Ocean. Pakistan's coastline is becoming a crucial staging post for China's takeoff as a naval power. . . . Pakistan's ports, which overlook some of the world's busiest shipping lanes, are key building blocks in a "string of pearls."
> (Khan 2017: 52, cited in Jackson 2018: 260)

Indeed, given the logistical problems outlined in the previous section with the notion of a goods transportation corridor from Gwadar to Kashgar, it is not clear what the commercial use of the port city is likely to be. Gwadar is in Balochistan, far from Pakistan's main commercial centres in Punjab and Sindh. Pakistan's main port is Karachi, several hundred kilometres to the east. Thus, the logic of establishing a port hub at Gwadar, given that Karachi already serves this purpose and is better connected to the populated interior of Pakistan, is not entirely clear. It is also a possibility, given that coal mines in Balochistan are being developed as part of CPEC, that Gwadar may be chiefly used by the Chinese in connection with the exploitation of local natural resources.

Nevertheless, problems with the development of Gwadar abound. Since 2004 there have been attacks in Gwadar by Baloch separatists which have resulted in the deaths of Chinese nationals (Boni 2016: 504). The result has been increased security measures which have effectively turned Gwadar "into a fortress with heavy security and frequent police and army checkpoints" (Boni 2019: 9). As a result of violence by Baloch and other separatists, approximately 32,000 Pakistani security personnel have reportedly been assigned to protect Chinese workers in Pakistan (Iqbal 2018: 209). An additional problem is that there have been protests by local fishermen against Chinese fishing vessels entering the waters around Gwadar (Aamir 2020). These issues, no matter how they are interpreted, demonstrate high levels of local alienation from the Chinese development of Gwadar port (Boni 2019: 9).

The CPEC megaproject is also encountering difficulties in terms of the availability of funding, a perpetual headache for the cash-strapped Pakistani government. In August 2020, a report based on "well informed sources" was published in a Pakistani business newspaper stating that Chinese financial institutions were reluctant to invest money in CPEC due to concern about "slow progress on CPEC projects" (Ghumman 2020). In addition, Saudi support for Pakistan's tottering economy seemed to waver in the summer of 2020 under the impacts of the coronavirus pandemic. Deferred payments for Saudi oil and loans as part of a US$6 billion bailout package agreed in 2018 were reportedly under threat as Riyadh reevaluated its options and contemplated greater cooperation with India (Stone 2020).

Prior to these events, in 2015 there had been a heated debate within Pakistan concerning the routing of the transportation corridor from Gwadar to Xinjiang. Controversially, the government decided to prioritise the construction of the more secure eastern route over the western one because existing road connections can be utilised instead of having to build from scratch (Iqbal 2018: 206). Thus, the construction as well as upgrading of transportation infrastructure in Punjab and Sindh provinces has been prioritised over the development of the economically less developed western provinces of Balochistan and Khyber Pakhtunkhwa. Most notably, a 392-kilometre motorway between Karachi and Lahore has already been completed. Another significant CPEC project is the upgrading of ML-1, the main railway line connecting Karachi with Lahore and Islamabad. A third is the New Havelian Dry Port being constructed to deal with the anticipation of increased freight traffic within CPEC. It is located near Islamabad. The decision to prioritise the eastern route has served to further antagonise citizens living along the undeveloped western route: in contrast to the progress made in the east, the transportation projects allotted to the west still linger in the feasibility study stage (CPEC 2021).

Apart from security issues, CPEC infrastructure construction projects, like other BRI projects, provide a partial solution to China's problem of excess domestic capacity in construction firms. Investing in Pakistan's energy and transport sectors provides work for Chinese companies. Long-term, building up Pakistan's economy would be good for China because it would develop the country as a market for Chinese exports and possibly a location for Chinese factories to use low-cost Pakistani labour. However, China's geopolitical calculation of the utility of giving Pakistan what it wants – better energy and transport infrastructure – in order to keep its Islamabad allies sweet and maintain the alliance against India certainly takes short- to medium-term priority over the possibly unrealisable long-term goal of developing Pakistan's economy.

2.6 Conclusion: deconstructing CPEC narratives

The analysis in this chapter has revealed that the discourse prevalent in much of the scholarly literature that CPEC is a 'game changer' and 'economic corridor' which will be able to negate the 'Malacca dilemma' conceals a range of other factors which influence its planning and implementation. These factors include regional geopolitics, internal security, and relations with India, as well as the reality of Pakistan's economic situation and the logistics of constructing infrastructure connecting Pakistan with its neighbours and the outside world.

First, there is the issue of the vagueness of the 'economic corridor' concept and the lack of a published large-scale feasibility or sustainability study in advance of the commencement of the project. Although of course important, this is not just a question of transparency. Without a clear advance conception and analysis of the issues involved in financing and connecting two countries through transport and other infrastructure, megaprojects of this type are likely to encounter logistical, economic, and political difficulties.

In the case of CPEC, the attempt to generate enhanced economic outcomes for both countries does not appear to have been planned with care. The ad hoc nature of the implementation of the megaproject is evident in such factors as the debate in 2015 over the prioritisation of the eastern or western route and the reported reluctance five years down the line of Chinese financial institutions to invest. It is also evident in the shifting of goalposts concerning the macro-level aims of CPEC. The core of the project has shifted from new cross-border infrastructure – which, apart from the fibre-optic cable, is not included among announced projects on the official CPEC website – to the construction of transport and energy infrastructure within Pakistan. Most extraordinarily, there is rarely (if ever) any mention of projects on the Chinese side of the border in any of the official publications or even in the scholarly literature. The focus is exclusively on projects within Pakistani territory. Therefore, there is no clarity or transparency about how the Pakistani projects are supposed to be integrated with Chinese ones – or whether this is even intended.

Alongside the planning problems is the associated problem of the lack of attention to the logistics and sustainability of cross-border infrastructure connections. The difficulty of the mountainous terrain, the tectonic fault line across which it lies, and the fact that the only existing road reaches China via a high-altitude pass which is closed in winter are all severe problems in themselves. However, there is also the issue of the border dispute with India. This affects the territory which connects Pakistan and China since it too is claimed by India. Any construction in the area is sensitive as far as India's relations with China and Pakistan are concerned. When the need to secure infrastructure against separatist attacks within Pakistan is added to the equation, the logistics and costs of constructing, securing, and maintaining cross-border infrastructure become even more difficult to assess.

An additional issue, rarely mentioned in the literature, is the environmental sustainability of CPEC projects, for which feasibility studies do not appear to have been done. Indeed, since the largest Chinese investment into CPEC energy projects is being committed to coal mines and coal-fired power plants (see Table 2.2), it is difficult to classify environmental sustainability as a primary goal of the megaproject. This is especially true since this issue is not prioritised in official publications or the media. Investment in coal-related projects officially amounts to over US$11.8 billion. The amount allocated to renewable energy projects is also significant at just over US$7.7 billion. However, most of this money (US$5.77 billion) is allocated to hydropower projects, which may themselves have considerable environmental impacts due to the damming of rivers. These potential impacts do not appear to have been evaluated in published environmental sustainability studies.

Another issue affecting CPEC is one that tends to be a characteristic of many Chinese projects: lack of transparency. When the details of financing are not made clear, doubts about corruption and cronyism tend to creep into the minds of observers. When leaders are appointed or removed without explanation, the public starts to suspect (probably correctly) that such hiring and firing is the result of behind-the-scenes machinations and leveraging of connections to obtain influence. Thus, when the head of the newly formed CPEC Authority is an ex-general, what comes to mind is the influence of the Pakistani military in the megaproject and the extent to which the Chinese played a role in the appointment. Having your megaproject run by the army at the behest of an outsized authoritarian neighbour is not a good look as far as persuading people of the 'win-win' benefits of the said megaproject is concerned.

In implementing a megaproject, it is desirable (although not necessarily achievable) for local communities to be supportive of the endeavour. In the case of CPEC, it is evident from the violent attacks on Chinese workers in Balochistan that sections of the local community feel excluded from the decision-making process. This is particularly true of the development of Gwadar port, where the high security, fortress-like set-up, and lack of transparency tell a tale of an enclave constructed without neighbouring communities in mind. The fact that the CPEC Authority is led by an ex-general also demonstrates a concentration of decision-making power in the Pakistani military-bureaucratic complex based in Punjab. In short, outsiders are forcing their decisions on Balochi and other communities without taking local needs into consideration.

Ultimately, CPEC is a flawed megaproject in terms of the assumed goals of cross-border 'economic corridor' connectivity. Numerous lessons can be learnt from CPEC concerning the planning and execution of other megaprojects, particularly those which involve cross-border connections between two or more nation states. Comparison of the official discourse on the idea of CPEC as a 'game changer' and solving the 'Malacca dilemma' with the reality of the megaproject's implementation reveals the incongruities outlined in this chapter. The lesson to be learnt here is that official discourse in the case of CPEC – but also in other officially endorsed large-scale economic initiatives – needs to be rigorously examined by observers with an air of healthy scepticism about stated objectives. The recycling of officially endorsed tropes in the media or by scholars is not conducive to the successful implementation of a project of any size, least of all an international megaproject.

In the case of CPEC specifically, scepticism is necessary concerning the frequently repeated assertion that the goals of the megaproject are solely economic ones. Without any doubt, the geopolitics of the Sino-Pakistani anti-Indian alliance loom large in the calculations of the generals and bureaucrats who run Pakistan, as well as the leaders of the PLA and the Chinese Communist Party

(CCP). Thus, scholars and practitioners who study and implement international megaprojects, even if they are concerned only with the technical aspects, need to be aware of concealed agendas and economic means being used to achieve political goals. As the CPEC case demonstrates, the motivations for implementing a megaproject may well be entirely different from what is stated in the official account.

References

Aamir, Adnan (2020) 'Pakistanis to Protest Arrival of Chinese Fishing Vessels', *Nikkei Asian Review*, 1 September. Available at: https://asia.nikkei.com/Spotlight/Belt-and-Road/Pakistanis-to-protest-arrival-of-Chinese-fishing-vessels (accessed 6 September 2020).

Abid, Massarrat, and Ayesha Ashfaq (2015) 'CPEC: Challenges and Opportunities for Pakistan', *Journal of Pakistan Vision*, Vol. 16, No. 2, pp. 142–169.

Afzal, Samrana, and Anum Naseem (2018) 'China Pakistan Economic Corridor (CPEC): Challenges and Prospects', *Pakistan Administrative Review*, Vol. 2, No. 1, pp. 209–222.

Ahmad, Muhammad Salman, Fahad Asmi, Madad Ali, Md. Mashiur Rahman, and Syed Mudasser Abbas (2017) 'China-Pakistan Economic Corridor: In the Context of "String of Pearl Strategy" ', *International Journal of Business and Social Research*, Vol. 7, No. 8, pp. 26–42.

Ahmar, Moonis (2015) 'Strategic Meaning of the China-Pakistan Economic Corridor', *Strategic Studies*, Vol. 34/35, No. 4/1, pp. 35–49.

Anwar, Zahid (2010) 'Gwadar Deep Sea Port's Emergence as Regional Trade and Transportation Hub: Prospects and Problems', *Journal of Political Studies*, Vol. 1, No. 2, pp. 97–112.

Bhutta, Zafar (2020) 'Pakistan Plans Second Phase of Pak-China Fiber Optic Cable', *The Express Tribune*, 20 February. Available at: https://tribune.com.pk/story/2160351/2-pakistan-plans-second-phase-pak-china-fibre-optic-cable.

Blanchard, Ben (2017) 'China Formally Opens First Overseas Military Base in Djibouti', *Reuters*, 1 August. Available at: www.reuters.com/article/us-china-djibouti-idUSKBN1AH3E3.

Boni, Filippo (2016) 'Civil-Military Relations in Pakistan: A Case Study of Sino-Pakistani Relations and the Port of Gwadar', *Commonwealth & Comparative Politics*, Vol. 54, No. 4, pp. 498–517.

Boni, Filippo (2019) 'Protecting the Belt and Road Initiative: China's Cooperation with Pakistan to Secure CPEC', *Asia Policy*, Vol. 14, No. 2, pp. 5–12.

Boni, Filippo (2020) *Sino-Pakistani Relations: Politics, Military and Regional Dynamics*, Abingdon, UK: Routledge.

Brunner, Hans-Peter (2013) 'What Is Economic Corridor Development and What Can It Achieve in Asia's Subregions?' Asian Development Bank Working Paper No. 117. Available at: www.econstor.eu/bitstream/10419/109610/1/wp-117.pdf.

Chaziza, Mordechai (2016) 'China-Pakistan Relationship: A Game-Changer for the Middle East?' *Contemporary Review of the Middle East*, Vol. 3, No. 2, pp. 1–15.

Chen, Aizhu (2020) 'PetroChina Strikes Big Gas Find in China Xinjiang's Junggar Basin: State Media', *Reuters*, 21 December. Available at: www.reuters.com/article/us-china-gas-discovery-petrochina-idUSKBN28V084 (accessed 25 May 2021).

China-Pakistan Economic Corridor (CPEC) Official Website (2021) Available at: cpecinfo.com (accessed 25 May 2021).

Erickson, Andrew S., and Gabriel B. Collins (2010) 'China's Oil Security Pipe Dream: The Reality, and Strategic Consequences, of Seaborne Imports', *Naval War College Review*, Vol. 63, No. 2, pp. 89–111.

Garlick, Jeremy (2018) 'Deconstructing the China-Pakistan Economic Corridor', *Journal of Contemporary China*, Vol. 27, No. 112, pp. 519–533.

Ghumman, Mushtaq (2020) 'Chinese Banks Reluctant to Fund CPEC Projects in Current Climate: Sources', *Business Recorder*, 26 August. Available at: www.brecorder.com/news/40014542 (accessed 5 September 2020).

Hussain, Zahid (2017, June) 'The China-Pakistan Economic Corridor and the New Regional Geopolitics', *Asie.Visions*, No. 94, Brussels: Institut français des relations internationals (Ifri). Available at: www.ifri.org/en/publications/notes-de-lifri/asie-visions/china-pakistan-economic-corridor-and-new-regional (accessed 15 May 2021).

Iqbal, Khuram (2018) 'Securing CPEC: Challenges, Responses and Outcomes', in Alessandro Arduino and Xue Gong (eds.) *Securing the Belt and Road Initiative: Risk Assessment, Private Security and Special Insurances Along the New Wave of Chinese Outbound Investments*, Singapore: Palgrave Macmillan.

Iwanek, Krzysztof (2019) 'No, Pakistan's Gwadar Port Is Not a Chinese Naval Base (Just Yet)', *The Diplomat*, 19 November. Available at: https://thediplomat.com/2019/11/no-pakistans-gwadar-port-is-not-a-chinese-naval-base-just-yet/.

Jackson, Steven F. (2018) *China's Regional Relations in Comparative Perspective: From Harmonious Neighbors to Strategic Partners*, Abingdon, UK: Routledge.

Khan, Muhammad Azam (2017) 'Pakistan's Port is Pivotal', *US Naval Institute Proceedings*, Vol. 143, No. 3, pp. 50–54.

Lam, Willy Wo-Lap (2015) *Chinese Politics in the Era of Xi Jinping: Renaissance, Reform, or Retrogression?* New York: Routledge.

Lanteigne, Marc (2008) 'China's Maritime Security and the "Malacca Dilemma" ', *Asian Security*, Vol. 4, No. 2, pp. 143–161.

Li, Xuanmin (2016) 'Gwadar Port Benefits to China Limited', *Global Times*, 23 November 2016. Available at: www.globaltimes.cn/content/1019840.shtml.

Liu, Zongyi (2015) 'Latest Progresses, Problems and Solutions of the "Belt and Road Initiative" in Southeast and Southwest Periphery of China' (Woguo "yidai yilu" changyi zai dongnan, xinan zhoubian de jinzhan xianzhuang, wenti ji duice, 我国"一带一路"倡议在东南、西南 周边的进展现状、问题及对策), *Indian Ocean Economic Studies* (Yìndùyáng jīngjì tǐ yánjiū, 印度洋经济体研究), Vol. 2015, No. 4, pp. 92–109.

Lu, Shulin (2014/2015) 'China Pakistan Economic Corridor: A Flagship and Exemplary Project of "One Belt and One Road" ', *Strategic Studies*, Vol. 34/35, No. 4/1, pp. 165–173.

Makhdoom, Atif Shan, Aisha Bashir Shah, and Kiran Sami (2018) 'Pakistan on the Roadway to Socio-Economic Development: A Comprehensive Study of China Pakistan Economic Corridor (CPEC)', *The Government: Research Journal of Political Science*, Vol. 6, No. 6, pp. 37–46.

Malik, Ahmad Rashid (2018) 'The China-Pakistan Economic Corridor: A Game Changer for Pakistan's Economy', in B.R. Deepak (ed.) *China's Global Rebalancing and the New Silk Road*, Cham, Switzerland: Springer, pp. 69–83.

Markey, Daniel S. (2020) *China's Western Horizon: Beijing and the New Geopolitics of Eurasia*, New York: Oxford University Press.

Marks, Michael P. (2011) *Metaphors in International Relations Theory*, New York: Palgrave Macmillan.

The Nation (2015) 'List of Pakistan-China MoUs', 21 April. Available at: https://nation.com.pk/21-Apr-2015/list-of-pakistan-china-mous.

Nawaz, Shuja (2008) *Crossed Swords: Pakistan, Its Army, and the Wars Within*, Oxford: Oxford University Press.

Noman, Omar (2009) *Pakistan: Political and Economic History Since 1947*, Abingdon, UK: Routledge.

Panda, Ankit (2015) 'Chinese State Firm Takes Control of Strategically Vital Gwadar Port', *The Diplomat*, 13 November. Available at: https://thediplomat.com/2015/11/chinese-state-firm-takes-control-of-strategically-vital-gwadar-port/.

Shah, Aqil (2014) *The Army and Democracy: Military Politics in Pakistan*, Cambridge, MA: Harvard University Press.

Siddiqa, Ayesha (2007) *Military Inc.: Inside Pakistan's Military Economy*, London: Pluto Press.

Siddiqui, Salman (2017) 'CPEC Investment Pushed from $55b to $62b', *The Express Tribune*, 12 April. Available at: https://tribune.com.pk/story/1381733/cpec-investment-pushed-55b-62b/.

Stone, Rupert (2020) 'Saudi Arabia's Special Relationship with Pakistan May Be on Borrowed Time', *Middle East Eye*, 13 August. Available at: www.middleeasteye.net/opinion/saudi-arabia-pakistan-special-relationship-under-threat.

Washington Times (2005) 'China Builds Up Strategic Sea Lanes', 17 January. Available at: www.washingtontimes.com/news/2005/jan/17/20050117-115550-1929r/ (accessed 6 September 2020).

Wolf, Siegfried O. (2016) 'The China-Pakistan Economic Corridor and Civil-Military Relations in Pakistan', *IndraStra Global*, Vol. 2, No. 4. Available at: www.indrastra.com/2016/04/PAPER-CPEC-and-Civil-Military-Relations-in-Pakistan-002-04-2016-0052.html.

Wolf, Siegfried O. (2020) *The China-Pakistan Economic Corridor of the Belt and Road Initiative: Concept, Context and Assessment*, Cham, Switzerland: Springer.

Yao, Yun (2015) 'The China-Pakistan Economic Corridor: A Risk Analysis' (Zhong ba jīngjì zǒuláng miànlín de fēngxiǎn fēnxi, 中巴经济走廊面临的风险分析), *South Asian Studies Quarterly* (Nányà yánjiū jìkān, 南亚研究季刊), Vol. 2015, No. 2, pp. 35–45.

Zhang, Chaozhe (2014) 'Building of China-Pakistan Economic Corridor: Opportunities and Challenges' (Zhōng bā jīngjì zǒuláng jiànshè: Jīyù yǔ tiǎozhàn, 中巴经济走廊建设: 机遇与挑战), *South Asian Studies Quarterly* (Nányà yánjiū jìkān, 南亚研究季刊), Vol. 2014, No. 2, pp. 79–84, 103.

3 Economic considerations

Image versus reality

3.1 Introduction: empirical data versus the 'game changer' and 'economic corridor' tropes

This chapter delves in more depth into two of the three main CPEC tropes discussed in Chapter 2: the established assumptions touted by many observers that CPEC is an 'economic corridor' and a 'game changer'. Both tropes are primarily about economics. The first is concerned with trade connectivity, especially via the overland link between China and Pakistan. The second refers to the potential transformation of Pakistan's economy via the stimulus provided by Chinese investments. Thus, in the first case there is a need to examine the empirical record of Sino-Pakistani trade before and during the CPEC era, while in the second case one ought to study the impact of CPEC investments on Pakistan's economic fortunes.

Hence, there are two aims in this chapter. The first is to assess the extent to which economic data confirm or invalidate the notion that CPEC has created or enhanced a hypothetical trade corridor between Pakistan and China, in the process producing favourable economic outcomes for both countries, and in particular Pakistan. The second is to evaluate the degree to which Pakistan's economy has been positively transformed since the advent of CPEC. To achieve these aims, the chapter analyses some primary data concerning Chinese investments in Pakistan, Chinese trade with Pakistan, and Pakistan's levels of public debt, comparing data in these areas from both before and after the inception of CPEC in 2015.

Since the name 'CPEC' prominently includes the words 'economic corridor', one would naturally expect the megaproject's central focus to be on enhancing trade between China and Pakistan, presumably, given the connotations of the 'corridor' label, by the overland route. On the Chinese side, one would expect there to be encouragement from the Chinese side for Pakistani exports across the land border in the form of incentives for Pakistani traders such as reduced tariffs, special economic zones, ease of obtaining travel and trade permits, and so on. Given these assumptions, it would be natural to expect there to be some results in the form of at least some degree of evidence of enhanced trade between China and Pakistan in the CPEC era. It would be reasonable to anticipate that Pakistan would have increased its volume of exports to China, or at least to be

DOI: 10.4324/9781003018377-3

on track to doing so. Given the 'win-win' rhetoric emanating from the Chinese side, there might also be signs of a reduction or at least slowing down of the rate of increase in Pakistan's trade deficit with China. On the other hand, if conditions for trade had really been enhanced, it is paradoxically likely that China would also be exporting more to Pakistan. At the very least, one would expect some tangible results in terms of enhanced mutual trade, with increasing volumes and ranges of goods being imported and exported. One would also expect, given the 'corridor' label, there to be larger volumes of goods traded between neighbouring Xinjiang province and Pakistan in both directions.

In what is inherently an asymmetrical partnership, one would also expect China, as the partner with serious cash reserves, to be investing substantially in Pakistan. China has more foreign exchange reserves than any other country, with over US$3.3 trillion in January 2021.[1] In contrast, Pakistan, a nation of over 200 million people, had just over US$20 billion in foreign exchange reserves in February 2021.[2] For comparison, this figure is only slightly more than that of impoverished Cambodia, which has a population of about 15.5 million people but reserves of over US$18 billion.[3] Given that Pakistan also had a national debt of 35.8 trillion rupees (US$228 billion) in November 2020 (Rana 2021), Pakistan's finances could be classified as in very poor shape indeed since foreign exchange reserves were equivalent to less than 10 per cent of national debt. For decades, Islamabad has lacked sufficient sources of ready finance to invest in its own economic development, in large part due to 'elite capture' from its corrupt and controlling elite classes (Gul 2018), but also due to general mismanagement of finances, frequently International Monetary Fund (IMF) loans, by incompetent administrations (Ahmad and Mohammed 2018: 235). According to the 'game changer' narrative, Chinese investments under the umbrella of CPEC were supposed to somehow change Pakistan's unfortunate status as an economic basket-case.

Thus, a supposed central goal of CPEC at the outset was for China to invest in Pakistan to boost Pakistan's economy, in large part by facilitating the construction of an 'economic corridor' connecting Gwadar to Xinjiang. Pakistan lacked energy and transport infrastructure, as well as the wherewithal to construct it. Therefore, one would expect China to have invested in these areas and at the minimum to have maintained the pace of investments throughout the years since CPEC's inception. One would expect so-called 'early harvest' investments to be transforming into results in terms of economic cooperation and Pakistan's economic growth. It would be anticipated that Pakistan would begin to see at least a certain amount of 'game-changing' economic benefits from the Chinese investments by the end of the first five years of the megaproject. However, given the presence of Pakistan's rent-seeking elites and the long record of failed IMF programmes (Ahmad and Mohammed 2018), it could also be anticipated that the story of Chinese investments was unlikely to be plain sailing. If it could be demonstrated that there was a lack of tangible improvements for Pakistan and sustained commitment from China over the first five years of CPEC, this finding would suggest that the BRI's 'flagship project' was not producing the results that were promised at the outset.

This chapter is thus an attempt to review some empirical evidence concerning Sino-Pakistani trade and Chinese investments in Pakistan to ascertain the extent to which CPEC has been a 'game changer' for Pakistan – and, perhaps to a lesser extent, for China. Trade and investment data from the CPEC era and before will be deployed to assess the degree to which CPEC projects have enhanced economic cooperation between the partners and Pakistan's economic development specifically.

3.2 Trade data

In examining trade between Pakistan and China, there is a rich trove of data in the annually published *China Statistical Yearbook* (2002–2019). This is fully accessible online. Of course, a frequent criticism made in the West is that Chinese data are incomplete and cannot be taken at face value. Nevertheless, as will be shown, the data covering the period 2001–2018 do not appear to sugarcoat asymmetries in trade relations between the two countries, and, in fact, do not paint a picture of enhanced trade in the CPEC era.

Figure 3.1 reveals China's trade with Pakistan from 2001 to 2018, in terms of total imports and exports from the Chinese perspective. At the beginning of the period, there is already evidence of a trade imbalance in China's favour, but the gap is far smaller than it was to become. During the next 17 years, Pakistan's trade deficit with China ballooned upwards, as Figure 3.2 reveals. Chinese exports to Pakistan constituted the vast majority of total trade volumes. Figure 3.3 shows that Pakistan's exports to China, taken as a percentage of total trade, shrank from over 40 per cent of the total in 2001 to under 12 per cent in 2018. The data therefore reveal that trade with China over the period from 2001 to 2018 negatively impacted Pakistan's balance of payments. It should be noted that a negative balance in this regard is not unique to Pakistan but is similar to the impact of trade with China on many other countries worldwide.

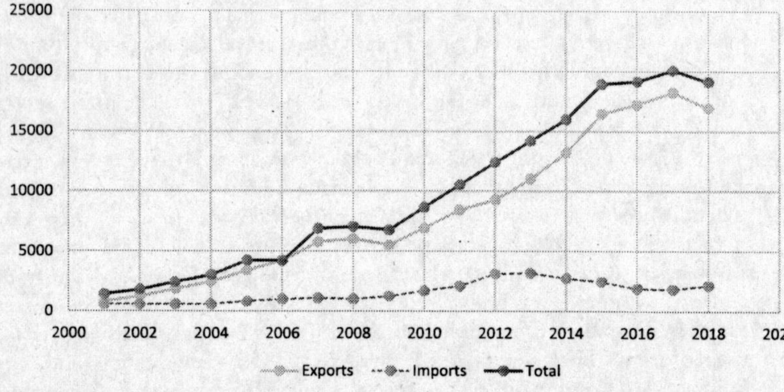

Figure 3.1 China's trade with Pakistan, 2001–2018 (US$ million)

Source: China Statistical Yearbook 2002–2019

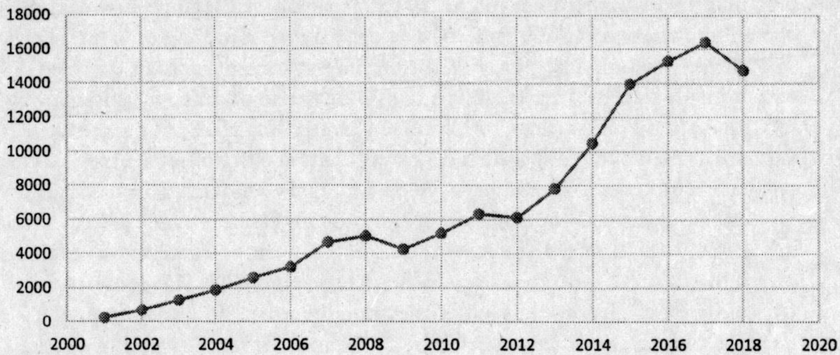

Figure 3.2 Pakistan's annual trade deficit with China (US$ million)

Source: China Statistical Yearbook 2002–2019

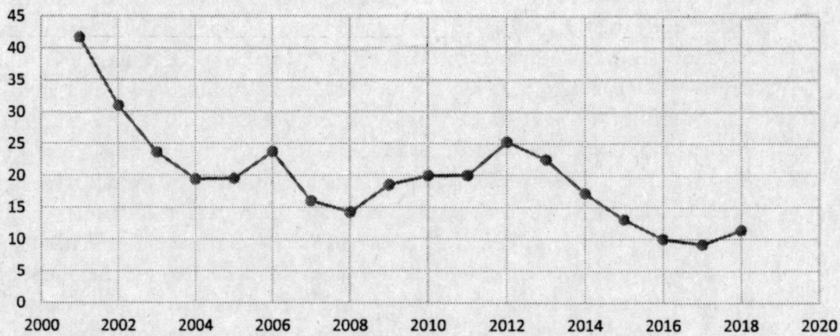

Figure 3.3 Pakistan's exports to China as percentage of total trade

Source: China Statistical Yearbook 2002–2019

On the other hand, the trade data do not present a clear picture regarding the impact of CPEC. Figure 3.2 shows that the imbalance favouring China mushroomed in the three years before CPEC was officially inaugurated in 2015. The rate of increase in the deficit then slowed in the next two years before dipping in 2018. However, with no data beyond 2018, it is impossible to know whether the 2018 dip represents a long-term trend or merely a temporary state of affairs. At the very least, it is not clear from the data that the advent of CPEC produced a dramatic shift in Pakistan's favour.

More significantly, if CPEC's 'economic corridor' would represent a 'game-changing' event for Pakistan's economy, one would expect an increase in overall trade. On the contrary, Figure 3.1 shows that in the years 2015 to 2018 overall trade volumes between China and Pakistan stagnated. The total trade in 2018 is only marginally higher than that in 2015. This comes after a dramatic increase in overall trade between 2009 and 2015, mostly due to a tripling of Chinese exports to Pakistan. In the same period, Chinese imports from Pakistan doubled, albeit with a steady decline after the 2013 high point. The decline in Pakistan's exports to China after 2013 appears to have been arrested in 2018; but since no further data are available it is impossible to know whether 2018 represents a sea change or just a temporary improvement. At any rate, the evidence is not suggestive of a dramatic increase either in overall trade or in Pakistan's exports to China in the CPEC era. In fact, the early CPEC years appear to represent a levelling-off in comparison to the six years which preceded CPEC. The trade data in the China Statistical Yearbook, such as they are, therefore do not support the 'game changer' rhetoric so often repeated by Pakistani scholars, media and officials.

It is difficult to get precise data on cross-border trade between Pakistan's border region of Gilgit-Baltistan (which is not classified by Pakistan as a province) and China's Xinjiang province. Nevertheless, field research by Rippa (2019, 2020) suggests that the advent of CPEC has had as many negative as positive impacts on small local traders due to increased regulation of the border connection. On the other hand, large-scale trade increased in 2019, with a reported 46.8 per cent increase in cross-border trade volumes compared to 2018 to a total of US856.3 million (Xinhua 28 December 2019). However, such a figure represents only somewhere between 4 and 5 per cent of the total China-Pakistan trade volumes for 2018 according to the 2019 edition of the China Statistical Yearbook.[4] This indicates that cross-border overland trade still constitutes a relatively small proportion of overall trade, most of the remainder of which is conducted by maritime routes, most notably via the port of Karachi (Rippa 2019: 259). Prior to CPEC, cross-border trade via the only available overland connection at the Khunjerab Pass using the Karakoram Highway constituted only around 4 per cent of overall trade volumes (World Bank 2011: 64). Thus, even the reported increase in trade volumes during 2019 does not appear to have substantially increased the proportion of overall trade passing by the overland route in comparison to the pre-CPEC era. In addition, the Asian Development Bank has repeatedly assessed the route from China and Central Asia across Pakistan to Gwadar and Karachi as more costly and time-consuming than other regional corridors (Asian Development Bank 2019: 26).

As regards the benefits of cross-border trade for merchants in the border regions, Rippa (2019: 259) notes that "Pakistani exports seem to have little impact on the economy of Gilgit-Baltistan." World Bank (2011) data reveal that many products sold in Xinjiang by local traders – such as clothes, sporting goods, and prayer mats – are not manufactured locally. Those that are – handicrafts, minerals, and herbs – are not sold in sufficient volumes to make much difference to the local economy and cannot make much of a dent in the overall trade deficit generated by the wide range of products imported to Gilgit-Baltistan from China's eastern provinces.

As for the utility of the cross-border transportation route for Chinese imports, the World Bank (2011: 67) has estimated the cost of shipping a container from Western China to Rawalpindi in Pakistan at about US$10,000. This compares unfavourably to the cost of transporting the same container overland through

China and then on to Pakistan by sea: the cost of the latter is estimated at around US$3,000–4,000. When one takes account of the fact that the Khunjerab Pass is closed for four months in winter due to heavy snowfall and is frequently shut down in summer due to landslides, security issues, and protests (Rippa 2019: 260), then the commercial value of the overland connection looks even more dubious.

A major blow to overland trade between China and Pakistan came in 2020, when the border remained closed for most of the year, apparently due to the coronavirus pandemic. This heavily impacted traders in Gilgit-Baltistan who rely on cross-border trade for their living (Nagri 2021). The border closed in November 2019 and reopened only briefly at wide intervals during 2020 for selected shipments. According to Pakistan customs officials, only 66 containers, mostly containing COVID-related equipment and other machinery, crossed from China to Pakistan during 2020 after the closure of the border (Nagri 2021). Only in August 2020 was the border "temporarily" reopened to allow some containers to pass through after being closed since March due to concerns about the spread of coronavirus (Abbas 2020).

Although, of course, the closure of the Khunjerab Pass arises from the situation revolving around the coronavirus pandemic, the almost complete closure of the border to trade in 2020 is surprising given the priority supposedly given by the Chinese to the development of the overland trade connection to Pakistan as a supposedly key part of CPEC. At the very least, even given the highly unusual circumstances, the 2020 closure is not indicative of sustained support for cross-border trade from the Chinese. The fact that trade almost totally halted in 2020, severely impacting local traders, certainly also casts doubt on the notion of CPEC's overland 'corridor' as a long-term economic 'game changer'.

3.3 Investment data

Despite its official inauguration in March 2015, CPEC was already in progress during 2014. The advent of CPEC accounts for the surge in the number and total volume of large Chinese investments in 2014 compared to 2013 (see Figures 3.4 and 3.5). However, new investments appear to have peaked in 2015, with a steady decline through 2016 and 2017 before surprisingly descending to lower than pre-CPEC levels in 2018 (see Figure 3.5). Investment volumes for the years 2019 and 2020 constitute an increase on 2018, but only to a similar level to that seen in 2010, without even accounting for the impact of monetary devaluation due to inflation over the decade. The high levels of investment by Chinese companies in Pakistan evident from 2014 to 2017 do not appear to have been sustained in the period from 2018 to 2020, and therefore tend to undermine the 'game changer' narrative to which many Pakistani scholars continue to adhere.

A combination of factors accounts for the fall in Chinese investments after the peak of 2015. First and foremost, there is the rationalisation of Chinese investments after the rush to comply with the goals of the BRI. Xi Jinping first presented the BRI in a broad way in autumn 2013, but the initiative's aims were only officially formulated in a document entitled *Vision and Actions on Jointly Building Silk Road Economic Belt and 21st-Century Maritime Silk Road*

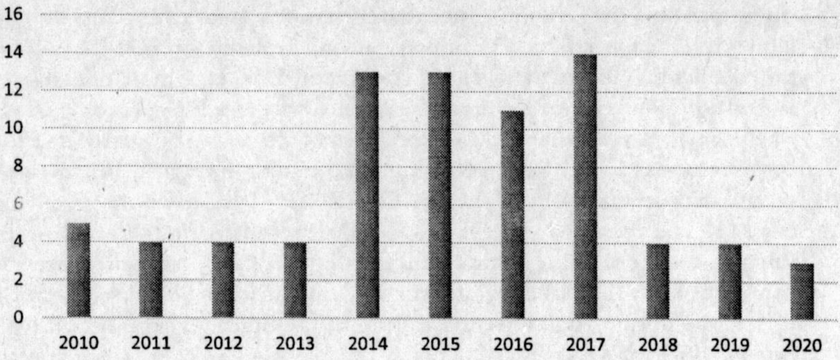

Figure 3.4 Number of large Chinese investment projects (US$100 million or higher) per year

Source: Scissors (2021), American Enterprise Institute's China Global Investment Tracker

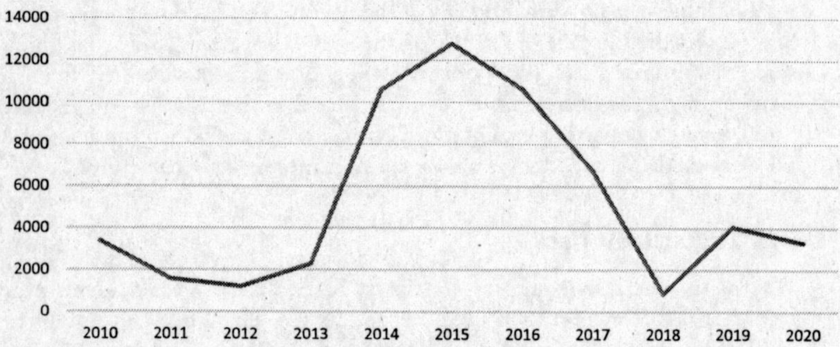

Figure 3.5 Annual Chinese investments in Pakistan, 2010–2020 (US$ million)

Source: Scissors (2021), American Enterprise Institute's China Global Investment Tracker

(National Development and Reform Commission (NDRC) 2015). The advent of CPEC thus roughly coincides with that of the BRI, with much discussion of the megaproject taking place prior to the official announcement during Xi's visit to Pakistan in April 2015. Since CPEC had been officially designated by the Chinese leadership as a 'flagship project' of the BRI by November 2014 (Ministry of Foreign Affairs of the People's Republic of China 2014), the pressure was on to ensure that initial investment levels matched the official rhetoric and justified the 'flagship project' designation – hence the rush by Chinese companies to fulfil expectations in 2014 and 2015. Once the initial enthusiastic rush was over, and it dawned on the Chinese leadership that a great deal of cash had been spent without considering the long-term utility of investments, companies were instructed to be more selective about how they spent their money – hence the 2017 drop-off and 2018 nadir.

From 2018 onwards, there appears to have been a reappraisal of the value of CPEC investments. Despite the global perception that China is pursuing 'debt-trap diplomacy' through BRI investments, Chinese companies, in fact, worry about recouping their investments in developing countries which often lack the wherewithal to repay loans and service interest payments. From 2018 onwards there is growing evidence of reduced Chinese faith in Pakistan's attractiveness as an investment partner as Beijing delays committing to new investments (Aamir 2021). While the cash-strapped Pakistani government continues to push for more funding, Chinese investments have lingered at pre-CPEC levels since 2018, with only slightly over US$3 billion in new large-scale investments committed in 2020 (Shakil 2020; Scissors 2021). This decline reveals the Chinese reluctance to commit large sums to projects which are apparently now viewed as suspect. The most obvious example of the slowdown in Chinese investments is Gwadar port, which was touted as a key CPEC project at the megaproject's launch.

3.4 Gwadar port

The development of Gwadar port has progressed more slowly than might have been anticipated, indicating that both Pakistan and China have been less committed to it than their initial, much publicised enthusiasm suggested. For instance, in 2015, the Minister for Ports and Shipping stated that the capacity of the port would be increased from 3 to 100 berths by 2045 (Tanoli 2015). However, six years later, in early 2021, the number of multipurpose berths had still not increased by even one extra berth (Gwadar Port Authority 2021). There is a lack of information as to why this is the case, but the lack of progress is obviously problematic in the context of the 'game changer' and 'economic corridor' narratives, as the analysis of the progress of Gwadar's infrastructure projects in the next section will also reveal.

During the early years of CPEC, there was relatively low usage of the port by commercial shipping. In September 2018, Pakistan's Ministry of Maritime Affairs submitted a report to the senate which stated that 99 ships from seven countries had docked at the port in the previous five years and that the weight of shipments was recorded as 1.439 million tonnes (Bahadur 2018). This implies that the annual weight of shipments between 2013 and 2018 was less than 300,000 tonnes per year on average. Gwadar's record in this regard fades into insignificance when compared to that of the country's main port at Karachi, which has 33 berths and handles about 26 million tonnes of cargo per annum (Karachi Port Trust 2019). A total of 1600 ships visit Karachi port annually, compared to a five-year average of around 20 ships per year docking at Gwadar between 2013 and 2018. Gwadar's total traffic in ships and cargo was therefore only a little over 1 per cent of Karachi's in the five years up to 2018. In addition, Karachi port's berth occupancy is calculated at about 45 per cent, meaning that there remains plenty of spare capacity (Karachi Port Trust 2019). Given Karachi's far better transport infrastructure and closer proximity to Pakistan's main population centres, as well as its clear potential for further growth, it seems illogical to present Gwadar as the main CPEC port rather than Karachi.

To hammer in the point about Gwadar's low usage and obviously problematic development over the first half-decade of CPEC, an eye-witness report by Bloomberg News in early 2021 suggested that usage of the port by commercial vessels was low or non-existent. After a visit to Gwadar, Bloomberg reporter Sheridan Prasso noted that Gwadar's three berths were empty apart from a Pakistan Navy frigate (Prasso 2020). Thus, given the existence of the already developed and busy Karachi port and poorly connected Gwadar's extremely underwhelming record, the latter's capacity to play a larger role in international trade is unproven at the time of writing. The record suggests that it is unlikely to be a 'game changer' in any meaningful sense.

As regards the 'economic corridor' trope, the N-10 653-kilometre Makran Coastal Highway to Karachi is the main road connection out of Gwadar in the direction of Pakistan's most populated regions. The construction of this road was completed during the Musharraf era, in 2004 (Frontier Works Organization 2010). The road reduced the journey from Gwadar to Karachi from the previous two days to only six or seven hours. Nevertheless, despite this reduction in transport time, it is not clear why there is any logical or logistical advantage in offloading cargoes at Gwadar instead of Karachi port only to transport goods by road to Karachi. It is also not clear that there has been any progress in building other transportation connections to the interior of Pakistan from Gwadar in the CPEC era via the so-called 'western route'. The start in December 2020 of a new project to build a barbed-wire security fence around Gwadar (Khan 2020) only adds to the sense that Gwadar is more an isolated outpost under threat from regional insurgency (see Chapter 4) than a central node in the China-Pakistan Economic Corridor. To compound the lack of real progress on transport infrastructure connecting the port to the rest of Pakistan, Gwadar's first airport had reportedly been under construction only since October 2019 and was not due to be completed until at least late 2022.[5]

In January 2019 there were reports that an oil refinery was to be built at Gwadar using investment from Saudi Arabia (Klasra 2019). However, two years later there had been no progress on this project. Instead, it was reported in February 2021 that Pakistan was inviting both China and Saudi Arabia to invest in an oil refinery at Hub, Balochistan, which is close to Karachi (Mustafa 2021). Thus, the project to install an oil refinery at Gwadar seemed to have been quietly dropped, while, at the same time, there was no certainty that Chinese companies would agree to participate in the construction of the Hub refinery.

Given Gwadar's evidently poor record so far in terms of playing a role in CPEC's 'economic corridor' trade between the Indian Ocean and Xinjiang province, it might seem logical to envisage a more limited role for the port primarily involving the development of impoverished Balochistan. However, recommendations that Gwadar be used for enhancing local trade in Balochistan rather than attempting to connect it to Central Asia have thus far been ignored by the government of Pakistan (Rafiq 2020). It seems that it is very difficult for those in authority in Pakistan to accept – since they have committed so much rhetoric to the narrative that Gwadar is an essential part of CPEC's 'economic corridor' – that they may have to revise Gwadar's role down from a 'game changer' for China-Pakistan trade to merely a regional port city.

3.5 Chinese-funded infrastructure projects

Since its inception, CPEC has mainly focused on Chinese-funded infrastructure projects in Pakistan. Thus, a good way of assessing the progress of the 'game changer' aspect of the megaproject is to evaluate the state of progress on individual infrastructure projects. Fortunately, this is relatively straightforward, because the official CPEC website outlines the state of progress on all projects classified as belonging to the megaproject (CPEC 2021). This section therefore focuses on an analysis of data obtained from the official CPEC website with the goal of qualitatively and quantitively assessing the extent to which CPEC's infrastructure projects contribute to developing Pakistan's economy and society. The primary aim is to continue evaluation of the 'game changer' trope, as well as secondarily to contribute some evidence to the examination of the 'economic corridor' and 'Malacca dilemma' tropes.

Although not explicitly formulated in this way on the official CPEC website, a standard way of classifying progress on construction projects is to classify the point reached in the project cycle (PC). PC-1 means the project is still in the feasibility study or review stage. PC-2 indicates that the project has advanced to the planning stage. PC-3 means that the project is in progress (under construction). PC-4 indicates that the project has been completed. A qualitative evaluation by the author of the description of progress on each of CPEC's 63 listed infrastructure projects reveals the information in Table 3.1.

The information in Table 3.1 reveals that the majority (44 out of 63) of official CPEC infrastructure projects are energy and transportation projects. This is not

Table 3.1 CPEC infrastructure projects

Type of project	*Number of projects*	*Completed (PC-4)*	*Under construction (PC-3)*	*Planning stage (PC-2)*	*Under review (PC-1)*
Energy	23	8	8	5	2
Transportation	21	5	3	5	8
Gwadar	8	2	4	0	2
Special economic zone	9	0	1	2	6
Communications technology	2	1	0	1	0
Total	63	15	16	14	18

Source: CPEC official website (author's analysis)

surprising, given the fact that one of CPEC's main goals is to address the lack of development in these two sectors. Pakistan needs to alleviate its chronic energy shortages in order to modernise its economy and improve people's living conditions (Malik 2018). It also needs better transport infrastructure to facilitate trade and connectivity both between regions and within cities. The focus on building energy and transportation infrastructure in Pakistan using Chinese capital and construction companies is therefore logical from the perspective of developing Pakistan's economy and society.

As stated in Chapters 1 and 2, it should be noted that there is no mention on the CPEC website of a project to construct cross-border oil and gas pipelines between Pakistan and China. Contrary to the assumption by numerous scholars that pipelines for transporting oil from Gwadar to Kashgar are planned (Irshad et al 2015: 203; Meng 2015: 37; Idrees et al 2018: 223; Ma 2018: 6; Qian et al 2018: 30; Raza et al 2018: 173; Wolf 2018: 86, 90; Alam et al 2019: 4; Hussain and Jamali 2019), there has been no mention of any cross-border pipeline project in official publications during the lifetime of CPEC. This issue will be examined in more detail in Chapter 4.

Table 3.1 reveals that fewer than a quarter of CPEC infrastructure projects were completed at the time of writing in March 2021. Of the various sectors of the megaproject, energy fared the best over CPEC's first six years, with eight projects completed and eight more under construction. Thus, there was tangible progress on over two-thirds of the promised energy projects. There had not been as much progress on transportation, close behind energy as the second most emphasised sector, since 13 out of 21 projects had not reached the construction phase. There was even less progress on special economic zones, with six out of nine projects still not even having reached PC-2, the planning stage. In communications technology, the completed project was a fibre-optic cable linking Pakistan to Xinjiang. Surprisingly, this was the only project out of the total of 63 to be focused on cross-border connectivity. Gwadar, classified as a special case deserving of its own category, had two completed projects, while four others were under construction. Given the supposed importance of the port for the implementation of CPEC's 'economic corridor' and the alleviation of the 'Malacca dilemma', it is surprising that the two projects still under review were the construction of breakwaters and the dredging of berthing areas and channels to allow vessels with larger drafts to dock.

Examining CPEC's energy projects in more detail (see Table 3.2) reveals specific areas in which progress has and has not been made. Of the eight projects which have been completed, four are projects involving the mining and production of energy from coal. The other four are wind farms. The production capacity of the four completed coal-powered projects is 4,620 megawatts (MW). The production capacity of the four completed wind-powered projects is 298 MW. In addition, there is also 400 MW of energy already being provided from the only partially complete Quaid-e-Azam 1,000 MW solar park. Thus, 5,318 MW of new energy production capacity has been added to Pakistan's energy supply by CPEC

Table 3.2 CPEC energy infrastructure projects (including cost)

Project	*Construction timeline*	*Installed energy production capacity (MW)*	*Estimated cost (US$ million)*	*Completed and operational (March 2021)*
2 × 660MW Coal-fired Power Plants at Port Qasim Karachi	2015–2018	1320	1912.2	Yes
Suki Kinari Hydropower Station, Naran, Khyber Pukhtunkhwa	2016–2022	870	1707	No
Sahiwal 2 × 660MW Coal-fired Power Plant, Punjab	2015–2017	1320	1912.2	Yes
Engro Thar Block II 2 × 330MW Coal-fired Power Plant and Surface mine in block II of Thar Coal field, 3.8 million tonnes/ year	2016–2019	660	2465.4	Yes
Hydro China Dawood Wind Farm (Gharo, Thatta)	2015–2017	49.5	112.65	Yes
300MW Imported Coal Based Power Project at Gwadar	2017-????	300	399.43	No
Quaid-e-Azam 1000MW Solar Park (Bahawalpur)	2016	1000	1301	No
UEP Wind Farm (Jhimpir, Thatta)	2015–2017	99	250	Yes
Sachal Wind Farm (Jhimpir, Thatta)	2015–2017	49.5	134	Yes
SSRL Thar Coal Block-I 6.8 mtpa & SEC Mine Mouth Power Plant (2 × 660MW)	2017–2023	1320	3212.12	No
HUBCO Thar Coal Power Project (Thar Energy)	2021	330	497.7	No
ThalNova Thar Coal Power Project	2021	330	497.7	No
Karot Hydropower Station	2015–2021	720	1698.26	No

(*Continued*)

Table 3.2 (Continued)

Project	*Construction timeline*	*Installed energy production capacity (MW)*	*Estimated cost (US$ million)*	*Completed and operational (March 2021)*
Three Gorges Second & Third Wind Power Project	2016–2018	100	150	Yes
CPHGC 1,320MW Coal-fired Power Plant, Hub	2017–2019	1320	1912.2	Yes
Matiari to Lahore 660kV HVDC Transmission Line Project and Matiari (Port Qasim) – Faisalabad Transmission Line Project	2016–2021	N/A	3158.34	No
Thar Mine Mouth Oracle Power Plant (1320MW) & surface mine	Unknown	1320	Unknown	No
Kohala Hydel Project, AJK	2018–2026	1100	2364.05	No
Cacho 50MW Wind Power Project	Unknown	50	Unknown	No
Western Energy (Pvt.) Ltd. 50 MW Wind Power Project	Unknown	50	Unknown	No
Azad Pattan Hydel Project, AJK	2026	701	1650	No
Phandar Hydropower Station	Unknown	Unknown	Unknown	No
Gilgit KIU Hydropower	Unknown	Unknown	Unknown	No

Source: CPEC official website, at http://cpec.gov.pk/energy (accessed 6 March 2021)

energy infrastructure projects. However, of this new energy production, almost 87 per cent comes from coal, while only about 13 per cent is derived from renewable energy. Thus, there must be a concern that the Chinese investments, while adding much-needed extra capacity to Pakistan's energy sector, have also added considerably to air pollution rather than alleviating it. In theory, it is commendable in theory that the stated focus of CPEC's 'early harvest' energy projects has been to ameliorate Pakistan's dire energy shortages as quickly as possible by exploiting a locally available energy source which had not been sufficiently developed previously (Malik 2018: 219). Nevertheless, the focus on coal means that these projects have added to environmental deterioration instead of developing sources of energy which would be more sustainable in the long-term, both for Pakistan and for the planet.

Of the eight energy projects which were under construction in early 2021, four were coal power projects, two involved hydropower, one was a solar park, and one was a transmission line project for delivering energy from coal-based power plants. The four coal projects, two of which were due to be completed in 2021, were intended to produce 2,280 MW of energy. The two hydropower projects, which were due to be operational in 2021 and 2022, were set to produce 1,590 MW of energy. The solar park, from which 400 MW of energy had been available since 2016, was supposed to produce 600 MW of additional energy once the second part of the plant was installed and operational. The total would be an additional 4,470 MW of power, of which slightly over half (51 per cent) would be produced from locally mined coal. Thus, while the picture regarding renewables appears better among this second group of projects which were under construction and were supposed to be online between 2021 and 2023, there was still a heavy preponderance of focus on coal-based power. Also, while the hydropower projects would contribute a renewable source of energy with no impact on air quality, the possible environmental impacts of damming rivers in the regions where the projects are located were unknown.

The remaining seven projects, which were in the planning or feasibility study phase, include four hydropower projects, two wind power projects, and just one more coal power project. However, only two projects (both hydropower) had received assigned budgets and completion dates (2026), so until such information becomes available, it is not possible to assess the remaining five in any meaningful sense. The two hydropower projects with assigned budgets were planned to have a total energy production capacity of 1,901 MW.

Overall, CPEC's energy infrastructure projects have so far added 5,318 MW of energy to Pakistan's energy grid. Another 6,371 MW of energy production is due to come online by 2026, making a possible total of 11,689 MW of additional power by that date. Given that Pakistan's total capacity in 2014–2015 – the start of CPEC – was 22,745 MW, this is indeed a potentially game-changing contribution of CPEC's energy projects, adding 51.4 per cent to total energy capacity. However, it should be recalled that 6,900 MW of the additional output would be generated by coal: 59 per cent of the total additional energy capacity. Of the remaining 4,789 MW of production, 3,491 MW would come from the damming of rivers. Only 1,298 MW – 11 per cent of the total – was due to be produced by solar and wind power. Thus, whatever the economic benefits to Pakistan of this additional energy output – which will be evaluated in the following section on Pakistan's economy – the environmental impacts and long-term sustainability of the energy projects must be a concern.

Progress on transportation projects has been slower than that in the area of energy. One rail and four road construction projects have been completed, but in 2021 a number of others were still in the planning or feasibility study stage. Surprisingly, further development of the Karakoram Highway, the only overland transport connection between Pakistan and China, was not included among CPEC projects. According to the official CPEC website (CPEC 2021), all transportation projects included in CPEC are internal to Pakistan, with no cross-border connectivity projects officially planned. As discussed in Chapter 2, no project to construct a China-Pakistan railway has been included among official CPEC projects. This refutes the assumption by some scholars (Cheng 2015: 5; Liu 2015: 99–100; Meng 2015: 37; Zhao and Liu 2017: 1; Qian et al 2018: 30), based on initial indications at the outset of the megaproject, that such a railway is really planned.

The most contentious CPEC transportation project is the expansion and reconstruction of Mainline-1 (ML-1), the 1,872-kilometre rail link between Karachi, Lahore, and Peshawar. This connection, once completed, will be a vital link between the commercial hubs of the country. It would also theoretically be vital to the implementation of CPEC's 'economic corridor' since the renovated ML-1 would run almost the length of Pakistan from the port of Karachi northwards. It is therefore surprising that work on the project has been delayed since a framework agreement was signed on 15 May 2017 when then Prime Minister Nawaz Sharif visited China.

The most serious problem besetting the ML-1 project is the question of funding. The project is budgeted at US$7.2 billion, of which the government of Pakistan was originally intending to seek US$6.1 billion from China. However, in November 2020 it was reported that there was a decision to ask for a reduced loan of US$2.7 billion from China "due to fears of overburdening the national economy" (Cuenca 2020). Still, even this loan had not been finalised by January 2021 due to a major disagreement on the interest to be paid: the Pakistanis were looking for an interest rate of less than 3 per cent, but this was not agreed by the Chinese (Chaudhury 2021a). In May 2021, the Chinese were still reportedly reluctant to advance any further loans for the ML-1 project (Chaudhury 2021b). With funding uncertain, the ML-1 project has been in limbo for years with no sign of light at the end of the tunnel.

In Gwadar, which has been given sufficient priority to be granted a dedicated section on the official CPEC website, only two out of eight projects had been completed by early 2021 – and one of these was a US$4-million master plan for Gwadar Smart Port City rather than an item of infrastructure. The other completed project is an expressway connecting the port to the Makran Coastal Highway. Other key projects, including Gwadar International Airport and the construction of breakwaters, berthing areas, and channels in the port itself, had not been completed. Thus, progress in developing the port of Gwadar, supposedly central to the 'flagship' CPEC megaproject, has been surprisingly slow and uncertain due to apparent Chinese reluctance to commit further funds without the certainty of loans being repaid.

3.6 Has CPEC been an economic 'game changer' for Pakistan?

Over the long term, Pakistan's economy has had severe structural problems relating to circular debt (Malik 2018: 224), insufficient foreign exchange reserves (Ahmad et al 2020: 647), inefficient taxation (Ahmad and Mohammed 2018: 244), and endemic elite corruption in the form of rent-seeking behaviours. Gul (2018: 196) has classified Pakistan's elite corruption as a form of "elite capture" in which national elites divert "resources designated for the benefit of the larger population." As a result of endemic long-term elite corruption and rent-seeking, Khan (2018: 259) notes that Pakistan has "myriad structural economic problems that continue to drag down its GDP growth rate". In these circumstances, the key question is therefore whether Chinese investments, many in the form of loans, are capable of transforming Pakistan's dire economic circumstances. In a nutshell, if elite capture continues and Chinese funds end up sustaining Pakistani elites' control of national agendas and affluent lifestyles rather than benefiting the national economy, then this would severely undermine the CPEC 'game changer' narrative.

At first sight, the 'game changer' narrative appears to make some sense. Chinese loans and investments would seem to provide the basis for a transformation of Pakistan's economy by funding energy and transportation infrastructure development by Chinese construction companies. However, if Pakistan is not able to service its debt due to lack of cash reserves and the rent-seeking behaviour of its elites, CPEC is likely to slow to a halt if China comes to believe that it will neither see much benefit from the investments nor recoup its cash. If China tires of its benefactor role and Pakistan's inability to repay Chinese loans, it may join the United States in reducing the flow of funds to Pakistan.[6]

Hurley et al (2018) identify Pakistan as one of eight countries at severe risk of debt distress due to loans taken from China under the umbrella of the BRI.[7] As already noted, Pakistan's federal debt was US$228 billion in November 2020 (Rana 2021). At the same time, foreign exchange reserves were only a little over US$20 billion in March 2021.[8] Ahmad et al (2020: 647) point out that Pakistan's inability to sustain sufficient levels of foreign exchange reserves to meet the country's financial obligations has resulted in recurrent economic crises which have repeatedly forced governments to seek bailouts from the IMF. Between 1988 and 2008, Pakistan received no fewer than 13 bailouts from the IMF, all but one of which "failed to meet the macroeconomic targets and were aborted" (Ahmad and Mohammed 2018: 235). Just one IMF assistance programme was judged to be a success, and that was only because the United States stepped in to provide financial assistance after 9/11: Washington needed to keep Pakistan onside in its 'war on terror' in neighbouring Afghanistan.

US economic assistance and military aid to Pakistan have followed a pattern of waxing and waning according to Washington's needs. For instance, aid was curtailed under the Carter, Bush (senior), and Clinton administrations in reaction to Pakistan's testing of nuclear weapons. However, US economic and military assistance spiked again after 9/11 since Washington needed Pakistan's cooperation or quiescence in its war against the Taliban across the border in Afghanistan (Center for Global Development 2013). After the war on terror spike in aid between 2002 and 2010, US assistance – most of which has been security-related rather than economic – steadily declined. Data published by the Congressional Research Service reveals year-on-year reductions in US assistance to Pakistan between 2014 and 2018. Economic-related payments to Pakistan totalled only US$84 million in 2018, down from US$608 million in 2014.[9] As US economic assistance dwindled towards zero, and it dawned on Pakistan's government that it could not rely on Washington, it is not surprising that Islamabad turned to China to fill the funding gap in the absence of any other willing lenders.

As discussed already in this chapter, the early CPEC years saw a boom in Chinese investments between 2014 and 2017 when Chinese companies were being encouraged to seek overseas opportunities under the umbrella of the BRI (see Figures 2.4 and 2.5). Yet, like the endless string of IMF loans and US economic assistance, Chinese capital does not appear to have turned around Pakistan's economic fortunes. The lack of positive outcomes straightforwardly explains Beijing's seeming reluctance to commit more funds to infrastructure investment, or at least to limit the flow of investment. Evidence of Chinese scepticism can be found in the unexplained delay to the planned development of Gwadar port and in the interminable discussions over interest rates on new Chinese loans (Aamir 2021).

Logically, if Pakistan demonstrates a long-term pattern of being unable to repay its debts and repeatedly seeking fresh loans to cover up the cracks in its economic structure, it does not make sense for a lender to keep pouring funds into what is clearly a financial black hole. At the same time, China's relations with Pakistan are based overwhelmingly on cooperation with Pakistan's elites. China's non-interference policy, restated endlessly and implemented throughout the world, involves supporting the existing regime within a country. CPEC, which has been organised through cooperation between Chinese and Pakistani civilian and military elites, has contributed to maintaining close Sino-Pakistani ties. Yet if Pakistan's 'elite capture' problem prevents the transformation of Pakistan's economy, this undermines the stated goals of CPEC – as well as the 'game changer' narrative. Instead of changing the game, CPEC has instead contributed to sustaining the status quo of excessive debt, elite corruption, and poor outcomes for Pakistan's economy and people.

As far as the infrastructure itself is concerned, it is also difficult to see much in the way of results. The single most important transportation project included in CPEC, the ML-1 rail link, was yet to be finished at the time of writing. Only 5 out of 21 transportation projects had been completed, and 13 remained at the planning or feasibility study stage (see Table 2.1). Even if the projects are completed, it is unclear whether they are sufficient to have a major impact on Pakistan's overall economic development. In an empirical study of the economic effects of CPEC, McCartney (2020) found little evidence that the megaproject's transportation projects would be sufficiently impactful to produce transformative effects on Pakistan's economy.

That leaves only CPEC's energy projects as a possible 'game changer'. Malik (2018: 225) notes that Pakistan needs to develop internal sources of energy to reduce its reliance on imports. Thus, the development of coal mines and coal-based power plants would seem to be a step in the right direction, particularly since coal has long contributed less than 6 per cent of Pakistan's energy needs (Malik 2018: 219). However, there are problems with the structure of Pakistan's energy supply system which reduce the effects of the increase in power generated by CPEC's coal power projects. Both Malik (2018: 224) and McCartney (2020: 3) note the crippling and persistent effect of circular debt on the electricity supply system. McCartney (2020: 3) explains:

> There are massive payment arrears at every stage of the generation, transmission, and distribution system. Consumer tariffs are insufficient to pay for the operation and functioning of the electricity system. This in turn increases arrears and suppliers of fuels and independent power producers go unpaid. This has undermined the viability of firms at every stage and their ability to continue functioning in the market.

With non-payments, theft of energy, and mismanagement also significant problems (Malik 2018: 224), it is difficult to see how the CPEC energy projects can contribute significantly to transforming Pakistan's economy without concurrent structural reforms which would address the issues. In the absence of such reforms (not evident so far), it is likely that the generation of more energy, while reducing energy shortages and the incidence of blackouts, will not be sufficient on its own to transform Pakistan's economic fortunes to the extent the 'game changer' narrative would anticipate.

3.7 Conclusion: reconfiguring tropes

This chapter has examined the 'game changer' narrative through analysis of several interconnected aspects of CPEC: trade, investment, Gwadar port, infrastructure projects, and Pakistan's economy. It has also, to a lesser but still significant extent, explored some empirical factors which weigh upon the 'economic corridor' narrative (these are analysed further in Chapter 4). The finding is that neither the 'game changer' nor the 'economic corridor' narratives are supported by the empirical evidence concerning Pakistan's economy and the implementation of CPEC's infrastructure investment projects.

The evidence presented in this chapter strongly suggests that CPEC, as it has been implemented so far (2015–2021), is not in any real (or even metaphorical) sense economically transformative for Pakistan. The available data point to the conclusion that Pakistan's economy has not yet been transformed in any meaningful sense by CPEC investments, chiefly due to ongoing structural problems which have not been addressed by the megaproject. These problems include circular debt, elite capture, inefficiencies of taxation, and the government's failure to diversify exports away from textiles (McCartney 2020: 27). Rather than transforming Pakistan's economic structures, Chinese investment programmes delivered under the labels of CPEC and the BRI have served to maintain Pakistan's political, economic, and military elites in their privileged positions, while bringing meagre benefits to the remainder of the population.

As far as CPEC's infrastructure investment projects are concerned, there have been some impacts, but far fewer than apparently envisaged at the outset of the megaproject. Most of CPEC's transportation projects, including at the port of Gwadar, remain unfinished or on the drawing board. The only cross-border project planned and implemented as part of CPEC is a fibre-optic cable connecting Pakistan to Xinjiang across the Khunjerab Pass. The overland transport connection between China and Pakistan is the same single highway, closed for four months in winter, that existed long before the advent of CPEC. No cross-border railway or energy pipelines are mentioned among official CPEC projects, not even at the feasibility study stage. The amount of cross-border trade remains unchanged, as does the number of berths in Gwadar port, which has been dealing with relatively low volumes of cargo compared to Karachi port. The one noteworthy impact of Chinese investment projects so far is to add extra output to Pakistan's energy grid. This is, of course, a not insignificant achievement, but since it has not been accompanied by necessary reforms to Pakistan's economic structure, the extra electricity output, while alleviating shortages and blackouts, is not on its own sufficient to transform Pakistan's economy.

In short, CPEC, as it has been implemented so far, is not a 'game changer' for Pakistan. McCartney (2020: 27) even goes so far as to conclude that the Chinese investment programme, even if it reaches the level of US$60 billion in total spread over 15 years, is too small (given the size of Pakistan's economy) "to make a transformative difference." Since Pakistan's government has failed to attempt a transformation of the national economic structure, "including the failure to diversify and upgrade exports away from simple textile products into more technologically demanding sectors" (McCartney 2020: 27), Chinese assistance provided through CPEC is on its own inadequate to affect game-changing results. And, as will be discussed further in Chapter 4, the implementation of a trade-enhancing 'economic corridor' connecting China and Pakistan overland has not been achieved either.

Notes

1 China State Administration of Foreign Exchange, Official Reserve Assets, January 2021. Available at: www.safe.gov.cn/safe/2021/0202/18181.html (accessed 2 March 2021).

2 State Bank of Pakistan, Domestic Markets & Monetary Management Department, Liquid Foreign Exchange Reserves. Available at: www.sbp.org.pk/ecodata/forex.pdf (accessed 15 March 2021).

3 International Monetary Fund, International Liquidity Selected Indicators: Cambodia. Available at: https://data.imf.org/regular.aspx?key=61545856 (accessed 2 March 2021).
4 National Bureau of Statistics of China, *China Statistical Yearbook 2019*, Section 11–5, 'Value of Imports and Exports by Country (Region) of Origin/Destination (2018)'.
5 CPEC official website, 'New Gwadar International Airport'. Available at: http://cpec.gov.pk/project-details/33 (accessed 27 February 2021).
6 Congressional Research Service, 'Direct Overt U.S. Aid Appropriations for and Military Reimbursements to Pakistan, FY2002-FY2020'. Available at: https://fas.org/sgp/crs/row/pakaid.pdf (accessed 16 March 2021).
7 The other seven countries at risk of debt distress due to BRI loans are: Djibouti, Kyrgyzstan, Laos, the Maldives, Mongolia, Montenegro, and Tajikistan (Hurley et al 2018: 11).
8 State Bank of Pakistan, Domestic Markets & Monetary Management Department, Liquid Foreign Exchange Reserves. Available at: www.sbp.org.pk/ecodata/forex.pdf (accessed 15 March 2021).
9 Congressional Research Service, 'Direct Overt U.S. Aid Appropriations for and Military Reimbursements to Pakistan, FY2002-FY2020'. Available at: https://fas.org/sgp/crs/row/pakaid.pdf (accessed 16 March 2021).

References

Aamir, Adnan (2021) 'China and Pakistan Fall Out Over Belt and Road Frameworks', *Nikkei Asian Review*, 19 January. Available at: https://asia.nikkei.com/Spotlight/Belt-and-Road/China-and-Pakistan-fall-out-over-Belt-and-Road-frameworks (accessed 2 March 2021).

Abbas, Ghulam (2020) 'Pak-China Trade Resumes Temporarily Through Khunjerab Pass', *Pakistan Today*, 5 August. Available at: https://profit.pakistantoday.com.pk/2020/08/05/pak-china-trade-resumes-tmporarily-through-khunjerab-pass/ (accessed 20 February 2021).

Ahmad, Ehtesham, and Azizali Mohammed (2018) 'Pakistan, the United States and the Bretton Woods Institutions: A Continuing Great Game?' in Aparna Pande (ed.) *Routledge Handbook of Contemporary Pakistan*, Abingdon, UK: Routledge, pp. 228–246.

Ahmad, Ishtiaq, Ali Azam, Khawaja Asif Mehmood, Muhammad Zahir Faridi, and Muhammad Aurmaghan (2020) 'Vulnerabilities of Developing Countries to Foreign Exchange Reserves and Remittances: A Case Study of Pakistan economy', *International Journal of Management*, Vol. 11, No. 8, pp. 646–659. Doi: 10.34218/IJM.11.8.2020.059.

Alam, Khalid Mehmood, Xuemei Li, and Saranjam Baig (2019) 'Impact of Transport Cost and Travel Time on Trade Under China-Pakistan Economic Corridor (CPEC)', *Journal of Advanced Transportation*, Vol. 2019, pp. 1–16. Doi: 10.1155/2019/7178507.

Asian Development Bank (2019) 'CAREC Corridor Performance Measurement and Monitoring: Annual Report 2019'. Available at: www.adb.org/sites/default/files/publication/619256/carec-cpmm-annual-report-2019.pdf (accessed 22 February 2021).

Bahadur, Irfan (2018) '99 Ships with 1.439 Million Ton Cargo Unloaded at Gwadar Port', *Customs Today*, 4 September. Available at: https://customstoday.com.

pk/99-ships-loaded-with-1-439-million-ton-cargo-unloaded-at-gwadar-port/ (accessed 23 February 2021).

Center for Global Development (2013) *Aid to Pakistan by the Numbers*, Washington, DC. Available at: www.cgdev.org/page/aid-pakistan-numbers (accessed 16 March 2021).

Chaudhury, Dipanjan Roy (2021a) 'China-Pakistan Embroiled in Major Disagreement Over CPEC Funding', *The Economic Times*, 25 January. Available at: https://economictimes.indiatimes.com/news/international/world-news/china-pakistan-embroiled-in-major-disagreement-over-cpec-funding/articleshow/80417000.cms?from=mdr (accessed 8 March 2021).

Chaudhury, Dipanjan Roy (2021b) 'China Reluctant to Lend $6 bn for Pakistan Infra Project', *The Economic Times*, 10 May. Available at: https://economictimes.indiatimes.com/news/international/world-news/china-reluctant-to-lend-6-bn-for-pakistan-infra-project/articleshow/82513333.cms (accessed 15 August 2021).

Cheng, Yunjie (2015) 'Research on Promoting China-Pakistan Trade Development Under the Background of "China-Pakistan Economic Corridor"' ("中巴经济走廊"背景下提升中巴贸易发展问题研究), *South Asian Studies Quarterly*, No. 2, pp. 94–101.

China-Pakistan Economic Corridor (CPEC) Official Website (2021) Available at: cpecinfo.com (accessed 25 May 2021).

Cuenca, Oliver (2020) 'Pakistan to Seek Reduced Chinese Loan for Mailine-1 Project', *International Railway Journal*, 18 November. Available at: www.railjournal.com/news/pakistan-to-seek-reduced-chinese-loan-for-mainline-1-project/ (accessed 7 March 2021).

Frontier Works Organization (2010) 'Makran Coastal Highway Project (MCHP)'. Available at: https://web.archive.org/web/20111004073704/www.fwo.com.pk/index.php?option=com_k2&view=item&id=176:makran-coastal-highway-project-mchp (accessed 27 February 2021).

Gul, Imtiaz (2018) 'Pakistan's Elite Capture and the State of Insecurity', in Aparna Pande (ed.) *Routledge Handbook of Contemporary Pakistan*, Abingdon, UK: Routledge, pp. 189–205.

Gwadar Port Authority (2021) 'Port Profile'. Available at: www.gwadarport.gov.pk/portprofile.aspx (accessed 23 February 2021).

Hurley, John, Scott Morris, and Gailyn Portelance (2018) *Examining the Debt Implications of the Belt and Road Initiative from a Policy Perspective*, Washington, DC: Center for Global Development.

Hussain, Mehmood, and Ahmed Bux Jamali (2019) 'Geo-Political Dynamics of the China-Pakistan Economic Corridor: A New Great Game in South Asia', *Chinese Political Science Review*, Vol. 4, No. 3, pp. 303–326.

Idrees, Rao Qasim, Rohimi Shapiee, and Haniff Ahamat (2018) 'Energy Cost Saving and Economic Prospective of China Pakistan Economic Corridor', *International Journal of Energy Economics and Policy*, Vol. 8, No. 6, pp. 217–226.

Irshad, Muhammad Saqib, Qi Xin, and Hamza Arshad (2015) 'One Belt and One Road: Dose China-Pakistan Economic Corridor Benefit for Pakistan's Economy?' *Journal of Economics and Sustainable Development*, Vol. 6, No. 24, pp. 200–207.

Karachi Port Trust (2019) 'Port Statistics'. Available at: https://kpt.gov.pk/pages/21/port-statistics (accessed 23 February 2021).

Khan, Feisal (2018) 'The Banking and Financial Sector of Pakistan', in Aparna Pande (ed.) *Routledge Handbook of Contemporary Pakistan*, Abingdon, UK: Routledge, pp. 247–261.

Khan, S. (2020) 'Gwadar: Why Is Pakistan Fencing China's Belt and Road Port?' *Deutsche Welle*, 20 December. Available at: www.dw.com/en/gwadar-why-is-pakistan-fencing-chinas-belt-and-road-port/a-56026436 (accessed 27 February 2021).

Klasra, Kaswar (2019) 'Saudi Investment in Gwadar Oil Refinery to Boost China-Pakistan Corridor Project', *Alarabiya News*, 23 January. Available at: https://english.alarabiya.net/business/energy/2019/01/23/Saudi-investment-in-Gwadar-oil-refinery-to-boost-China-Pakistan-Corridor-project (accessed 27 February 2021).

Liu, Zongyi (2015) 'China's "One Belt, One Road" Initiative in the Southeast and Southwest: Current Status, Problems and Countermeasures of the Surrounding Development' (我国"一带一路"倡议在东南、西南周边的进展现状、问题及对策), *Research on Indian Ocean Economy* (印度洋经济体研究), Vol. 2015, No. 4, pp. 92–109.

Ma, Bei (2018) 'China-Pakistan Under the Framework of "One Belt One Road": Research on Security Risk Prevention' ("一带一路"框架下中国- 巴基斯坦:安全风险防范研究), *World Religious Cultures*, No. 3, pp. 29–34.

Malik, Atta Ali (2018) 'From Chaos to Building a Secure, Sustainable Energy Future', in Aparna Pande (ed.) *Routledge Handbook of Contemporary Pakistan*, Abingdon, UK: Routledge, pp. 206–227.

McCartney, Matthew (2020) 'The China-Pakistan Economic Corridor (CPEC): Infrastructure, Social Savings, Spillovers, and Economic Growth in Pakistan', *Eurasian Geography and Economics* (online first, 26 October). Doi: 10.1080/15387216.2020.1836986.

Meng, Liaokuo (2015) 'Pakistan's Strategic Position from the Perspective of "One Belt One Road: Analysis of Its Realization Path' ("一带一路"视野下的巴基斯坦战略地位及其实现路径探析), *Forum of World Economics & Politics*, No. 4, pp. 29–45.

Ministry of Foreign Affairs of the People's Republic of China (2014) 'Li Keqiang: Building the China-Pakistan Economic Corridor Flagship Project', 8 November. Available at: www.fmprc.gov.cn/mfa_eng/topics_665678/ytjhzzdrsrcldrfzshyjxghd/t1209089.shtml (accessed 20 February 2021).

Mustafa, Khalid (2021) 'Pakistan Offers China Partnership in $9b PARCO Coastal Refinery', *The News*, 8 February. Available at: www.thenews.com.pk/print/786888-pakistan-offers-china-partnership-in-9b-parco-coastal-refinery (accessed 27 February 2021).

Nagri, Jamil (2021) 'Closure of China Border Brings Economic Woes for GB People', *Dawn*, 11 January. Available at: www.dawn.com/news/1600923 (accessed 20 February 2021).

National Development and Reform Commission (NDRC) (2015) *Vision and Actions on Jointly Building Silk Road Economic Belt and 21st-Century Maritime Silk Road*, 28 March, issued by the National Development and Reform Commission, Ministry of Foreign Affairs, and Ministry of Commerce of the People's Republic of China, with State Council Authorization. Available at: https://reconasia-production.s3.amazonaws.com/media/filer_public/e0/22/e0228017-7463-46fc-9094-0465a6f1ca23/vision_and_actions_on_jointly_building_silk_road_economic_belt_and_21st-century_maritime_silk_road.pdf (accessed 21 February 2021).

Prasso, Sheridan (2020) 'One of China's Most Ambitious Projects Becomes a Corridor to Nowhere', *Bloomberg*, 2 March. Available at: www.bloomberg.com/news/

features/2020-03-02/a-china-belt-and-road-project-becomes-a-corridor-to-nowhere (accessed 5 March 2021).

Qian, Hongdao, Sonia Azam, and Hamid Mukhtar (2018) 'China Pakistan Economic Corridor: Legal Injunctions and Protection of Chinese Investments in Pakistan Under OBOR Initiative', *European Journal of Research in Social Sciences*, Vol. 6, No. 2, pp. 29–37.

Rafiq, Arif (2020) *Regional Transit Trade Isn't Enough to Drive Pakistan's Gwadar Port*, Washington, DC: Middle East Institute, 14 October. Available at: www.mei.edu/publications/regional-transit-trade-isnt-enough-drive-pakistans-gwadar-port (accessed 22 February 2021).

Rana, Shahbaz (2021) 'Public Debt Jumps Rs3.7tr in a Year', *The Express Tribune*, 19 January. Available at: https://tribune.com.pk/story/2280474/public-debt-jumps-rs37tr-in-a-year (accessed 23 February 2021).

Raza, Hasan, Ahmed Osama, and Samreen Hena (2018) 'China Pakistan Economic Corridor (CPEC): The Counter Balancer of Momentous Energy Crisis in Pakistan', *Advances in Social Sciences Research Journal*, Vol. 5, No. 7, pp. 172–180. Doi: 10.14738/assrj.57.4841.

Rippa, Alessandro (2019) 'Cross-Border Trade and "The Market" Between Xinjiang (China) and Pakistan', *Journal of Contemporary Asia*, Vol. 49, No. 2, pp. 254–271.

Rippa, Alessandro (2020) 'Mapping the Margins of China's Global Ambitions: Economic Corridors, Silk Roads, and the End of Proximity in the Borderlands', *Eurasian Geography and Economics*, Vol. 61, No. 1, pp. 55–76.

Scissors, Derek (2021) *China Global Investment Tracker*, Washington, DC: American Enterprise Institute (AEI). Available at: www.aei.org/china-global-investment-tracker/ (accessed 21 February 2021).

Shakil, F.M. (2020) 'China Slowly Retreating from Pakistan's Belt and Road', *Asia Times*, 26 December. Available at: https://asiatimes.com/2020/12/china-slowly-retreating-from-pakistans-belt-and-road/ (accessed 3 March 2021).

Tanoli, Qadeer (2015) 'Gwadar Port to Have 100 Berths by 2045: Minister', *The News*, 27 June. Available at: www.thenews.com.pk/print/48058-gwadar-port-to-have-100-berths-by-2045-minister (accessed 21 February 2021).

Wolf, Siegfried O. (2018) 'China-Pakistan Economic Corridor (CPEC): Regional Cooperation in the Wider South Asian Region', in B.R. Deepak (ed.) *China's Global Rebalancing and the New Silk Road*, Singapore: Springer, pp. 85–100.

World Bank (2011) *Gilgit Baltistan Economic Report: Broadening the Transformation*, Washington, DC: World Bank Open Knowledge Repository.

Xinhua (2019) 'Trade Volume Surges at China-Pakistan Border', *Xinhuanet.com*, 28 December. Available at: www.xinhuanet.com/english/2019-12/28/c_138663671.htm (accessed 20 February 2021).

Zhao, Jie, and Liu Ning (2017) 'China-Pakistan Economic Corridor Connects to China: The Impact of Import and Export Trade – Counterfactual Simulation Based on Industry-Level Data from Countries Along the Route' (中巴经济走廊贯通对中国进出口贸易的影响 – – 基于沿线国家产业层面数据的反事实模拟), *World Economic Research* (世界经济研究), No, 3, pp. 123–133.

4 A pipeline too far? Logistics, mountains, and the 'Malacca dilemma'[1]

4.1 Introduction: theoretical considerations concerning the 'Malacca dilemma'

This chapter dissects the 'Malacca dilemma' trope in more depth in connection with the logistics and geopolitics of the hypothetical oil pipeline connection between Gwadar and Xinjiang. It assesses the viability of a pipeline connecting China to the Indian Ocean through Pakistan via a close analysis of evidence obtained from both primary and secondary sources. The aim is to deepen the analysis by applying a similar treatment to the 'Malacca dilemma' trope and the question of a cross-border pipeline as that applied in the previous chapter to the 'game changer' and 'economic corridor' tropes. The analysis is framed using some theoretical considerations concerning the re-assertion of the vital role that geography plays in geopolitics, based on the work of Cohen (2015), as well as Grygiel (2006) and Brewster (2017). This physically centred approach contrasts with that of critical geopoliticians such as Ó Tuathail (1996), who emphasise the "discursive/representational construction of geographic space" (Brewster 2017: 270). Cohen's approach is not set up in opposition to critical geopolitics, however, but rather as an attempt to re-emphasise the importance of physical geography for the study of geopolitics.

In developing Cohen's approach, I take as a key discussion point David Brewster's assertion that the establishment by China of overland connections to the Indian Ocean would radically transform the geopolitics of the IOR by opening up to Chinese influence what has been until now a closed geographical space which India has been attempting to dominate. If China becomes a major actor in the IOR, he points out, the consequences for the region are hard to predict amid radically altered geopolitical dynamics (Brewster 2017). However, as the analysis in this chapter will reveal, it is highly doubtful that China is even intending to enhance the tenuous connection of Xinjiang with the Indian Ocean via enhanced transportation and pipeline networks.

This chapter is therefore intended to be a rich, empirically grounded study based on close analysis of data (to the extent that it is available) concerning the economic and logistical viability of constructing overland transportation and pipeline connections between the Indian Ocean and China's landlocked Xinjiang

DOI: 10.4324/9781003018377-4

Uyghur Autonomous Region (XUAR) via Pakistan. To examine the proposed CPEC connections, the analysis takes as a starting point Brewster's geographically based investigation of the geopolitics of the route from China through Pakistan to the Indian Ocean, expanding on it by adding analysis of factors relating to logistics, economics, and security. This is done in order to dig beneath the surface of official announcements and optimistic media reports to ascertain the feasibility, according to hard data, of establishing a land corridor between Gwadar and Xinjiang. Information is obtained from an in-depth analysis of primary sources such as the Gwadar Port Operating Authority's website and Chinese state-supported news media such as the newspaper *Global Times*, as well as secondary sources such as journal articles and policy papers.

Although there are limitations, enough information can be obtained to strongly suggest that China's primary motivation for involvement in Pakistan is geopolitical rather than geo-economic. The reality of the proposed overland pipeline and transportation corridor transforming trade between China and Pakistan is that it is more a symbol of cooperation than a fully achievable goal. The argument presented here, based on the empirical evidence, is that the primary aims of China's engagement in Pakistan are to secure its restive border regions (including Xinjiang and Tibet) and to balance against its regional rival India by establishing and maintaining a Chinese presence in Pakistan and the IOR. The author proposes to call the type of balancing used by China in the IOR, which is based on a long-term strategic assessment of physical geography, *geopositional hedging*.

The concept of geopositional hedging is partly based on traditional Chinese notions of geographical space. William Callahan notes, for instance, that the underlying basis of Zhao Tingyang's agenda-setting *tianxia* theory, which is taken from traditional Chinese philosophy, is geographical (Callahan 2008: 751; Zhao 2006). It is developed, as Henry Kissinger (2011: 23–25) points out, from the tactics of encirclement used in the Chinese game of *weiqi* (called *go* in Japan). *Weiqi* is a popular Chinese strategic board game involving attempts to encircle the opponent or to resist encirclement by the opponent by putting down black or white stones. Geopositional hedging is a system of putting down marker 'stones' in key geographical positions – such as Gwadar, Hambantota in Sri Lanka, and Kyaukpyu in Myanmar – for potential future use, for example in case of possible conflicts. The aim is for China to strengthen its long-term geostrategic position vis-à-vis rivals (in this case India) without great risk or, despite appearances to the contrary, excessive financial expense. Thus, China's approach involves hedging strategically against future risk: China has used a strategically hedged approach to secure long-term oil supplies from the nearby Persian Gulf by maintaining good relations simultaneously with both Iran and Saudi Arabia, who are bitter regional rivals (Garlick and Havlová 2020). Hence, since China's strategic planning also involves establishing a physical presence in littoral and other territories it deems to be of strategic importance, this specific aspect of its strategic hedging in the IOR region can be termed geopositional hedging.

The chapter thus begins with an extended assessment of the background to and prospects for the CPEC land corridor, based mainly on an in-depth analysis of primary and secondary sources relating to CPEC's conception and funding, the port of Gwadar, the physical geography separating Pakistan and China, security issues, and pipeline logistics. The sources reviewed suggest that Chinese investment in CPEC pipelines is less likely to go ahead than some commentators appear to believe, due to economic, logistical, geographical, and security problems which are acknowledged by some Chinese experts. The final sections then assess China's motivations for involvement in Pakistan. The evidence included in this chapter points, above all, to Chinese interest in offsetting its rival India's regional dominance in South Asia through a strategy of geopositional balancing in Pakistan and other nations (such as Myanmar and Sri Lanka) in the Indian Ocean littoral.

4.2 The CPEC 'land corridor' problem defined

In assessing CPEC's ostensible aim of enhancing connections between Pakistan and China's northwestern Xinjiang region, it is important to outline problems relating to the physical topography and geographical location of the China-Pakistan border region. In particular, the Karakoram Highway which connects the two countries, built with great difficulty between 1959 and 1979 and now under reconstruction, passes through difficult mountain terrain and an earthquake zone. As already mentioned, this territory is claimed by India, meaning that any further development of the region is geopolitically sensitive. It is also potentially a transit point for Islamic insurgents such as the East Turkestan Islamic Movement (ETIM) and other groups seeking the independence of the Chinese province of Xinjiang.

There are also further problems to be solved in the remainder of Pakistan. The poor condition of most Pakistani infrastructure (for instance in the field of energy) and the lack of Pakistani financial resources demand massive Chinese investment with uncertain economic outcomes and doubts concerning Pakistan's ability to repay loans. In addition, amid frequent regional insurgencies and other outbreaks of violence, there is the difficulty of maintaining security around infrastructure investment projects such as the construction of factories, plants, railways, and pipelines – and, as the construction of a security fence begun in December 2020 demonstrates, in Gwadar (Khan 2020).

Based on an observation which was made by Chinese President Hu Jintao in 2003 (and which has been reiterated so often by numerous commentators that it has become something of a truism: see for instance Yang and Siddiqi 2011: 574–575; Hartpence 2011: 586; Chaziza 2016; Jash 2016: 100), one of the principal motivations for China's involvement in Pakistan is to establish an alternative to the usual maritime trade route via the Straits of Malacca and the South China Sea (SCS) (Lanteigne 2008: 143–144). In this interpretation, the Straits of Malacca is considered a 'chokepoint' because it is a stretch of water which could hypothetically be blockaded, thus preventing vital supplies of oil and other commodities from reaching China. The point is frequently made in both the energy security literature and elsewhere that approximately 80 per cent of China's oil supplies pass through the Straits of Malacca and the SCS on their way to Eastern

China: this is termed, per Hu's coinage, the 'Malacca Dilemma' (Lanteigne 2008: 143–144). However, Leung (2011: 1334) is not alone in suggesting that "the so-called Malacca Dilemma has been commonly exaggerated." Already prior to the advent of CPEC a second authoritative study supported his point that the danger of blockade or piracy is not as serious as it has often been said to be, since alternative sea routes can easily be found in case of disruption at Malacca and blockading all of these routes would require a massive and costly deployment of naval resources (Erickson and Collins 2010).

In economic terms, a peer-reviewed study in a major energy journal claims that the overland route through Pakistan to Xinjiang is shorter and potentially cheaper than the sea route (Shaikh et al 2016). It could therefore save time and money as well as providing China with enhanced energy security. The fact that Gwadar is located on the Persian Gulf across the waters from Oman and the United Arab Emirates (where the Chinese oil company Sinopec owns 50% of the oil terminal at Fujairah) and next to Iran is suggestive (cartographically at least) of an intention to transport at least some crude oil into China via CPEC along with other resources and goods. The question then is whether the Chinese intention would be to construct oil and gas pipelines to Xinjiang along the lines of the recently constructed Myanmar-China pipelines, or whether fuel could instead be viably transported by road or a new railway. However, critics doubt whether oil and gas transported via pipelines would really be cheaper than using the maritime route (Erickson and Collins 2010; Leung 2011). In addition, since large quantities of fossil fuels already pass via existing pipelines through Xinjiang on their way from Central Asia, there logically seems little need to add to these supplies at present. Since Xinjiang is also "China's largest gas producing and second largest oil producing region and has one of the largest networks of oil and gas pipelines in China" (Yang and Siddiqi 2011: 575), the rationale for adding extra fossil fuels via a logistically difficult and probably expensive route is not clear.

The literature on CPEC which has appeared since the announcement of China's investment in April 2015 reveals that there appears to be a surprising lack of clarity and consensus to date about the practical feasibility of connecting Gwadar and Xinjiang. For instance, the study by Shaikh et al (2016) referenced at the beginning of the previous paragraph set out to study the prospects for oil being transported northwards to China from Gwadar. However, despite a detailed quantitative cost analysis, the authors did not even mention the feasibility of a hypothetical pipeline in terms of non-economic issues such as the logistics of construction in the physical geography of the Himalayas, security issues relating to terrorism, the necessity of building through disputed territories in the north of Pakistan, and capacity issues relating to Gwadar port. This is not the only article in a peer-reviewed journal to make the (unfounded) assumption that the geographically shorter distance to China from the Persian Gulf to Xinjiang via Pakistan must automatically mean cheaper oil: Chaziza (2016: 4) is among those who repeat this idea without examining the data in sufficient depth.

Another incorrect claim (citing a Reuters news item which does not mention the data supposedly cited) which appears in a peer-reviewed journal article is that "[a]s a direct consequence of the huge investment by China, Gwadar port contains 13 berths and has the capacity to hold bulk carriers of 350,000 deadweight tonnage" (Amirthan 2016: 89). Examining the reality of Gwadar port's present capacity on the Gwadar Port Authority's website in February 2021 reveals that its capacity is currently much less than this, with three functioning multipurpose berths and the capacity to accept vessels of up to 50,000 deadweight tonnage (DWT) only.[2] Remarkably, this represents no advance at all on the situation in 2017 (Garlick 2018: 523), indicating that little substantial work was done on developing the port from 2018 to 2020. The three existing berths were all completed in 2005 in the so-called Phase I of the project to expand the port. As of March 2016, according to the Pakistani Minister for Ports and Shipping, work on the further berths which were supposed to constitute 'Phase II' had not yet begun (Express Tribune 2016). Andrew Small confirms that from 2007 onwards, for a variety of reasons, including the removal of Pervez Musharraf from office in 2008, acrimony surrounding alleged mismanagement by the Port of Singapore Authority (which had been granted the contract to run the port in 2007 but which withdrew from the project in February 2013 after extended bouts of litigation), and security issues relating to the safety of Chinese workers, "very little of 'Phase 2' was ever undertaken" (Small 2015: 101).

The confusion surrounding Gwadar and Sino-Pakistani relations since the launch of CPEC in 2015 means that there is a pressing need to further clarify the state of play today. As Small (2015: 95–96) puts it, "for a long time the story of the economic relationship between the two sides has been one of excitable headlines touting large numbers, ports, pipelines, and energy transit routes followed by frustration, disappointment, stalled projects, and much smaller figures buried away in statistical reports." A central aim of the remainder of this chapter is thus to assess the feasibility of CPEC acting as a transportation corridor for crude oil and other commodities and goods from the IOR to Xinjiang in western China. The analysis is based on an examination of the primary data available (such as it is), as well as evidence provided in secondary sources, including ones which predate the advent of CPEC.

4.3 From Gwadar to Kashgar, the hard way

Gwadar is located in Balochistan, in the southwest of Pakistan. It is on the Arabian Sea opposite Oman and to the east of the Straits of Hormuz. About 70 kilometres to the west is the Iranian border, on the other side of which is the port of Chabahar, now being developed by India. Approximately 650 kilometres to the east of Gwadar, along the Makran Coastal Highway (construction of which was completed by China in 2004), is Pakistan's main port, Karachi, which is part-owned by China Harbor Engineering Company (CHEC).

Gwadar was a fishing village under Omani rule until 1958, when the enclave was purchased by Pakistan for US$3 million (Small 2015: 100). Plans to build a deep-sea port were initiated in 1993, and construction began in 2002 using Chinese finance and labour (Willasey-Wilsey 2016). Phase I of the project was completed in 2007, whereupon the administration of the port was handed over to the Port of Singapore Authority (PSA International) on a 40-year lease. However, PSA withdrew by mutual consent from this deal in 2012–2013, and the rights to administer the port until 2047 were sold to COPHC in May 2013.[3] PSA's withdrawal came ostensibly because Pakistan refused to transfer 584 acres of land under the control of the Pakistani Navy, although problems with security due to local Baloch militants have also been cited as an associated reason (Fazl-e-Haider 2012).

One major impediment to Gwadar's utility as a port is geographical. Gwadar is relatively isolated from Pakistan's major population centres, and Balochistan is one of Pakistan's poorest provinces. Apart from the highway to Karachi there is at present little else of note in the vicinity of the port in terms of infrastructure. Pakistan's main industrial centres are far away in Gujranwala, Faisalabad, and Lahore (Boni 2016: 512). For this reason, there has been an extended debate within Pakistan about whether the proposed connection from Gwadar to the Chinese border should take an eastern or western route (or both) (Raza 2016; Usman and Sikander 2016). Each route would likely encounter numerous logistical problems, and each has already met with objections from factions within the country.

Either way, linking Gwadar to China overland demands crossing the entire length of Pakistan, including the Karakoram mountains in the north. The Karakoram Highway, completed in 1979, crosses into China through the Khunjerab Pass, at an altitude of 4,693 metres. Topographical maps, photographs, and tourist films reveal that the pass, located on the border, is wide, but the road which winds up to it through Pakistani territory is precariously cut into the mountainside above the Khunjerab river, which is the headwaters of the Hunza river. As the highway passes from the Khunjerab Pass down into Pakistan, its "main geomorphic features include hanging valleys, waterfalls, glaciers, snow-fields, lateral and terminal moraines and cirques" (Negi 1991: 86–87). In other words, this is extremely difficult terrain for the building and maintenance of pipelines. Sections of the highway are subject to frequent landslides and rockslides since it crosses a geological fault line where the Eurasian and Indian plates collide. More than a thousand Pakistani and Chinese workers died during the construction of the highway due to landslides (Small 2015: 99). A major landslide in 2010 caused the closure of a section of road due to the formation of a new lake, until the completion in 2015 of 24 kilometres of bridges and tunnels which restored the road link. The geological instability of Pakistan's northern region allied with difficult terrain, high altitudes, the possibility of insurgency, and the fact that the border region is disputed with India mean that adding any further infrastructure alongside the highway (such as a railway or pipeline) is fraught with risk and extreme difficulty in terms of maintenance and construction, including extensive high-altitude tunnelling.

The prohibitive cost of constructing high-altitude pipelines is another factor against the proposed project. In November 2016, Mei Xinyu, a Chinese Academy of International Trade and Economic Cooperation research fellow and representative of the Chinese Ministry of Commerce, commented to the state-endorsed newspaper *Global Times* that since high-altitude pipelines "need extra heating and insulating equipment as well as high-power pumping stations" to pump fuel uphill, the costs of transporting oil over the Himalayas to Xinjiang would be approximately 16.6 times higher than the conventional route from Saudi Arabia to Eastern China by tanker (Li 2016). Mei concluded that "[f]or the same amount of investment, it's more economically viable to build very large crude carriers than oil pipelines." Comparative analysis conducted by Erickson and Collins (2010: 92) reveals that oil transported by pipeline from Angarsk in Russia to Daqing in northern China via relatively flat terrain is around double ($2.41 per barrel) that of oil transported from Saudi Arabia to Ningbo ($1.25 per barrel), even though the distance covered is less than half (3,200 km versus 7,000 km). This indicates beyond reasonable doubt that the cost of fuel transported through the proposed CPEC pipelines would be substantially higher than that transported by existing routes. This contradicts the assertion to the contrary made by some scholars (for instance, Idrees et al 2018) that the CPEC route can be cheaper than the standard maritime route through the Straits of Malacca and the South China Sea to ports on China's eastern seaboard.

Another question surrounds the draft (defined as the dredged depth) of Gwadar port. As previously stated, the port can currently receive vessels up to 50,000 DWT, with a draft of 12.5 metres. Gwadar has three 200-metre berths plus a 100-metre service berth.[4] This capacity is insufficient to receive even mid-sized cargo carriers and oil tankers, severely limiting the utility and commercial success of the port at present.[5] Further dredging of the approach channels and port is scheduled, but so far the depth to be dredged has not been specified.[6] Since all models of large cargo carriers and oil tankers are over 200 metres in length and have drafts of between 16 metres and 35 metres, to receive even those of medium size the entry to Gwadar port needs not only to be dredged further but its berths also need to be extended or new ones built.[7] According to the official CPEC website, as of early February 2017, COPHC's draft business plan for port improvements was still under review by the Pakistani Ministry of Ports and Shipping.[8] Wu Minghua, a shipping analyst, also noted that Gwadar Port had a handling capacity of 1 million tonnes per year in 2016, while China's total oil imports were 335.5 million tonnes in 2015, further casting doubt on the practical value and cost-effectiveness of offloading and transporting oil supplies by this route (Li 2016).

A further problem for both Gwadar and CPEC is security. The security situation in Pakistan has been highly unstable for years, with terrorism and regional insurgencies producing violent attacks across the nation, not least in Balochistan, "an area over which Islamabad's political hold has weakened substantially since 2007" (Hartpence 2011: 598). Three Chinese engineers were killed in a 2004 bomb attack at Gwadar by Baloch separatists, and nine more were injured (Small 2015: 102). In 2017, a Chinese couple was kidnapped in Quetta by separatists and eventually killed (Masood 2017). Due to ongoing sporadic attacks by Balochi separatist forces, the construction of a security fence around Gwadar began in

December 2020 (Khan 2020), indicating that the port city's security was seen as an ongoing issue. The issue of Gwadar's shaky security situation undermines its practical utility, explaining also why a project to build an oil refinery financed by Saudi Arabia (Klasra 2019) had apparently been re-envisaged as a plan to develop a similar facility at Hub in the easternmost part of Balochistan close to Karachi (Mustafa 2021).

The remainder of Pakistan is also not noted for its safety. Indeed, more Chinese were targeted in terrorist attacks in Pakistan between 2004 and 2010 than anywhere else in the world (Duchâtel 2011: 543). There were further attacks on Chinese nationals, including a group of engineers, in 2013, resulting in several fatalities (Small 2015: 171–173). The security situation became so unstable that the Pakistani cricket team played almost all its 'home' matches in the United Arab Emirates for an entire decade after a terrorist attack on the visiting Sri Lankan team in 2009 due to fears of further violence (Selvey 2012).

The difficulty of ensuring security means that constructing any hypothetical transportation and pipeline corridor to China which crosses the length of Pakistan is a risky enterprise demanding a high level of security manpower and placing a heavy load on the Pakistani armed forces. Exacerbating these concerns as far as China is concerned is the possibility of Islamic insurgents crossing into restive Xinjiang from Pakistan. Indeed, China tightened security at the Khunjerab Pass in January 2017 in an attempt to prevent militants from entering Chinese territory (Dasgupta 2017). There was also an upsurge in violence inside Pakistan in the first two months of 2017, with Pakistani security forces seen as struggling to cope (Khattak 2017). In short, it is far from clear that CPEC could provide a more secure route for fossil fuels from the IOR to China than the existing maritime one via Malacca. Indeed, it would be more likely to add to China's energy security headache rather than to alleviate it.

An alternative solution for connecting Gwadar to Xinjiang is to cross the nearby border into Iran and/or Afghanistan and then go through the Central Asian states of Turkmenistan and Kazakhstan (Chaziza 2016: 8–9). Three gas pipelines originating in Turkmenistan already supply natural gas to China, so there might be a possibility of linking Gwadar with Turkmenistan via a more secure route at lower altitude, although it is not clear that this would make any economic or logistical sense. An alternative proposal for a Turkmenistan-Afghanistan-Pakistan-India pipeline (TAPI) is already on the table but is reportedly beset with difficulties and delays (Michel 2017). In 2015, with the lifting of sanctions on Iran, an Iran-Pakistan gas pipeline to be built by China was proposed. This is intended to pass through Gwadar on its way to Nawabshah in south-eastern Pakistan (Shah 2015). As of November 2016, the Iranian section of the pipeline was reportedly already constructed, but construction of the Pakistani section was delayed due to the lack of funds on the Pakistani side (Graeber 2016).

All in all, there are a number of serious logistical problems facing the hypothetical project of enhancing Gwadar to Xinjiang connections by adding to the existing road link. While the upgrading of the Karakoram Highway continues, proposals for pipelines and a railway have not yet got off the drawing board, and the absence of references to them in Chinese media since 2017 suggests that they are likely to have been quietly shelved. Pakistan appears to be constantly short of hard currency and dependent on Chinese loans or investment, implying that China will have a near-monopoly on decision-making in CPEC. This means that if the Chinese government and Chinese companies decide that certain aspects of CPEC are not economically viable, they will not be funded. Given the fact that a Chinese state newspaper has reported serious Chinese doubts about the profitability of supplying oil through pipelines to Xinjiang (Li 2016), and since even Pakistani experts have expressed doubts about Gwadar's economic viability (Boni 2016: 512), it seems unlikely that such a difficult project will find a place high on China's list of potential investments in the foreseeable future. The comments of two Chinese experts in *Global Times* undermine the assertion of Shaikh *et al.* that an oil pipeline is cost-effective and feasible. They also confirm that Gwadar Port does not at present have the capacity to transfer oil from tankers to shore in anything other than relatively small quantities (Li 2016; Shaikh et al 2016).

4.4 A salutary tale: lessons from the China-Myanmar pipeline

China's first attempt to bypass the Malacca 'chokepoint' in the wake of Hu Jintao's 2003 comments took shape in 2004 when talks were opened with Myanmar on constructing an oil pipeline to Kunming. Then in December 2005 a contract between the then Burmese government and PetroChina to deliver 6.5 trillion cubic feet of natural gas to Yunnan over 30 years was signed (Storey 2006). Interest in exploiting the Shwe gas field drove the project to its next stage, and agreements to build both natural gas and oil pipelines were drawn up in 2008 and 2009. Construction of the crude oil pipeline commenced on 31 October 2009 (Xinhua Economic News 2009).

The project consists of two pipelines (one for natural gas and one for crude oil), constructed between 2009 and 2014, which pass in parallel through Myanmar on their way to Kunming in China's southwestern Yunnan province. The gas pipeline, which originates at Kyaukpyu port, is intended to exploit the Shwe gas field in the Andaman Sea, while the oil pipeline begins at a new deepwater port on nearby Maday (or Made) Island, at which tankers from the Middle East can dock and offload crude oil (Meyer 2015). While the gas pipeline has reportedly been in operation since October 2013 (Shin 2013), the oil pipeline took longer to build, was 'essentially completed' in early 2015, but was beset by delays, questions concerning economic viability, and disputes over terms (Chen and Aung 2016; Myint and Gloystein 2017). The fact that, according to Chinese state media, the first delivery of oil from a tanker occurred only in April 2017 underlines the fact that the oil pipeline lay unused for more than two years after its construction was completed (Cao and You 2017; Cao and Shan 2017; Bloomberg News 2017). A proposal to construct a railway along the pipeline route between Kunming and Kyaukpyu was also put forward, but this was cancelled by the Myanmar government in July 2014 due to the pressure of negative public opinion concerning perceived Chinese exploitation of Myanmar's resources (Pasick 2014).

The two pipelines reportedly cost a total of US$2.45 billion to build. However, while the gas pipeline began pumping fuel after its completion, the 771-kilometre oil pipeline lay unused during 2015, due, according to a Myanmar Oil and Gas Enterprise official, to a number of reasons, including the following: disagreements over fees and taxes, probably due to the fact that the Myanmar government had changed between drawing up the contracts and the completion of the pipeline; the fact that construction of the refinery at the Yunnan end of the pipeline which was due to process the crude oil had not been completed; and low oil prices making operations unprofitable (Pasick 2014). Even after the completion of the Yunnan refinery in July 2016, oil did not start pumping until 2017 due to continuing disputes over the level of taxes to be paid by China, revealing this to be a central reason for the ongoing delay: the Myanmar government wanted an extra 5 per cent tax on top of the earlier agreed transit fee and pipeline tariff (Chen and Aung 2016). A tanker which was due to deliver oil to Kyaukpyu for the first time in March 2017 was unable to deliver its load due to yet another breakdown in negotiations between PetroChina and the Myanmar government (Myint and Gloystein 2017). After the first delivery in April 2017, oil started flowing through the pipeline in early May (Reuters 2017), and 2 million tonnes were transferred in the four months to September (Chan 2017). However, the cost of the oil is high, with Myanmar set to collect $13 million per year from China as a Right-Of-Way (ROW) easement payment, plus two custom duties, whose exact amount has not yet been decided (Chan 2017). It is also important to note that the tankers delivering crude to Kyaukpyu port for the transfer would otherwise take the oil to ports in mainland China where there would be no payments or duties. Thus, the costs associated with the running of the pipeline cast doubt on its economic efficacy.

The reaction to the Chinese pipelines in local Myanmar communities has also impacted their operation to a degree. The widespread civic protests which led to the cancellation of the railway project from Yunnan to Kyaukpyu in 2014 may have been a factor in the delay to the commencement of the operation of the oil pipeline: local inhabitants were outraged that they had not been consulted and had not benefitted from the pipelines, and also that energy resources were being diverted to China when most of Myanmar lacks electricity (Pasick 2014). Then, in early 2017, violence between Buddhists and the minority Muslim Rohingya group in the state of Rakhine, which includes Kyaukpyu port and the pipelines, put the operation of the Chinese enterprises in further doubt (Ding 2017). An article by a freelance Burmese photojournalist in November 2015 reveals a picture of growing disillusionment among local people on Maday Island concerning the economic benefits of the Chinese-funded oil pipeline and terminal (Yu 2015).

It is not possible at this stage to assess the impact on the pipelines of local protests and complex outbreaks of sectarian violence in firmly quantitative terms. However, it can be stated that the Chinese involvement with successive Myanmar regimes means that the pipelines have a political and social impact which demands further research since it affects the local environment within which the pipelines are operated. These issues have also added an extra layer of insecurity to the Chinese energy security equation rather than significantly alleviating the situation.

In short, the problems inherent in the China-Myanmar pipeline project are surely instructive as regards the potential construction of a pipeline between Gwadar and Kashgar. Indeed, the remarkable Chinese capacity for learning valuable lessons from failed projects in a timely fashion (according to Deng Xiaoping's dictum of 'crossing the river by feeling for the stones') appears to have led in late 2016 to China quietly shelving CPEC's pipeline project in the customary low-key manner adopted by the Chinese authorities when dealing with failure, disappointment or tragedy: without fanfare or publicity.

4.5 If not pipelines, then what is CPEC for?

If the notion of constructing pipelines (and perhaps also a railway) from Gwadar to Kashgar appears impractical, as the previous analysis suggests, then four questions need answering. First, why is China involved in Gwadar? Second, what does China hope to gain from CPEC? Third, what are China's overall intentions with regard to its 'all-weather friend' Pakistan? And fourth, what does Pakistan expect from China?

It is likely that the answers to all these questions are interlinked. It is also likely, given the complexity of the issues involved, that, as the authors of a 2016 study put it, "China's motives in pursuing CPEC are variegated" (Rifaat and Maini 2016). Filippo Boni, who conducted field research in Pakistan, concurs in stating that security, economics, and foreign policy are "inextricably intertwined when it comes to the development of the port of Gwadar and, by and large, Pakistan-China relations" (Boni 2016: 500). However, the argument developed in this section is that China's involvement in Gwadar – and Pakistan as a whole – is primarily motivated by considerations of geopolitics based on physical geography (geopositional hedging), particularly with respect to the most significant nation located in the IOR, India, and it is this which brings China and Pakistan's interests into alignment.

Geopositional hedging differs from balancing strategies – such as classical hard balancing, soft balancing, and offshore balancing – in that the strategic actor, in this case China, prioritises geographical factors. Classical hard (or external) balancing involves states forming military alliances to ensure that stronger states do not achieve a dominant position, while in soft balancing weaker states employ economic and diplomatic means to equalise their position vis-à-vis a potentially hegemonic state. Offshore balancing, as outlined by John Mearsheimer and Stephen Walt (2016), is a strategy recommended for the United States specifically: it entails encouraging allies to build up their own defences instead of the United States maintaining an onshore military presence. In contrast with balancing strategies, China's geopositional hedging aims to establish physical footholds in selected countries (in this case Pakistan and Myanmar) with a view to establishing a stronger long-term geostrategic position with regard to a regionally more powerful rival (in this case India). The aim of geopositional hedging, in this conception, is neither to build up onshore military bases nor to remain entirely offshore, but instead to establish a non-military presence at selected sites (such as commercial ports). These can be maintained long-term for the purpose of keeping a powerful rival geopolitically honest by making it aware of the incoming actor's presence. At the same time, onshore economic investment and infrastructure building give the hedger influence in the host country by building up a degree of soft power through enhanced economic connections.

In this reading of the situation, Gwadar is a geostrategic 'place marker' or, as Henry Kissinger would have it, a metaphorical *weiqi* stone: the utility of the 'stone' may not yet be clear, but Beijing appears to believe that it is better to seize the opportunity (Kissinger 2011: 23–25). If China intends to be an actor of significance in the IOR and South Asia, as well as to shore up its existing position, it needs to hedge against Indian activity (for instance investment in Chabahar port along the coast in Iran) as well as the US naval presence in the region (based in Diego Garcia). Given that India and China have not exactly had close relations since the 1962 border war between them, and amid ongoing territorial tensions along their extended frontier, including Indian claims on the Karakoram territory which connects Pakistan with China geographically, China seeks to ensure that it has as many strategic footholds in the region as possible (Yang and Siddiqi 2011: 575). US intentions in the region have been unclear in recent years, but there is always the chance that the Americans will re-engage: China therefore needs to hedge against that possibility as well.

Viewing China's port-building programme in the IOR as geopositional hedging permits a more nuanced understanding of Chinese activity than simple aggression or hard balancing. In essence, China intends to establish a physical presence to enhance its overall long-term defensive security rather than aiming to directly challenge or threaten India, a goal which is currently unrealistic in terms of maritime power projection, particularly given the continuing American military presence in the IOR. The nuclear rivalry between Pakistan and India and the ongoing Sino-Indian border tensions contribute to the assessment that geopositional hedging in Gwadar is a strategy which is intended to serve China's long-term security interests in the sense of what China terms 'active defence'.[9]

In this light, it is, of course, to be expected that China refutes claims that it is out to 'encircle' India despite suspicions on the Indian side. On the other hand, extended supply lines which stretch for thousands of kilometres from China's southernmost naval base on Hainan Island mean that China's PLAN is not yet able to rival India's navy in the IOR (Lanteigne 2008: 148). China's geopositional strategy takes account of this fact by attempting to gradually build up a network of commercial ports around the IOR. At the same time, occasional activity from the PLAN, such as a visit by Chinese warships to Karachi in June 2017, remains relatively low key (Neelakantani 2017).

This is not to say that what can be termed China's port-of-entry strategy has been entirely smooth sailing. Not all efforts by China to incorporate ports in other

IOR countries into its so-called 'string of pearls' have come to fruition, and even those that have are often controversial. For instance, a Chinese bid to develop a port in Bangladesh was quietly rejected in 2016 by the Bangladeshi authorities, probably due to behind-the-scenes pressure from India, the United States, and Japan, which had already been developing a port (Bagchi 2016). Two Chinese port construction projects in Sri Lanka, at Colombo Port City and Hambantota, have developed in fits and starts as Sri Lankan governments have come and gone (or changed policy). Concerns about Chinese loans being converted into Chinese equity and ports potentially being used for military purposes have not been eased by Chinese insistence that the investments are purely commercial in nature, as a senior Indian scholar has noted (Singh 2017). Stopovers in Sri Lanka by Chinese submarines have understandably led to Indian howls of protest, with a 2017 proposed docking rejected by Sri Lanka under pressure from India (Aneez and Sirilal 2017). The Sino-Indian geopolitical rivalry in the IOR means that all Chinese port projects stir suspicion on the part of India, as well as other regional actors, most notably the United States and Japan. Such considerations explain why India also continues to reject Chinese invitations to join the BRI.

Several observers who have interviewed or maintain contacts with Chinese foreign policy makers have noted that according to their sources China's long-term priority in Pakistan has been to prioritise security concerns over economic ones (Ye 2009; Small 2010; Duchâtel 2011). Duchâtel's anonymous source, interviewed in 2009, reveals China's long-term geopolitical strategy with regard to Pakistan and so is worth quoting in full:

> If projects progress too slowly or if they are threatened by insecurity, it's easy: we stall them. The energy-and-trade corridor has only little importance and security costs are high. Pakistan has no resources, no gas, no oil, ***only a geographical position*** [italics added]. Pakistan insists that China should invest in this project, but China is now a market economy and seeks returns on [its] investments. China was considering the construction of this corridor under Musharraf because there was a sufficient degree of security and economic growth, but today it is meaningless.
>
> (Duchâtel 2011: 557)

Another area in which China seeks to enhance its security in Pakistan is the aforementioned issue of containing threats to the stability of Xinjiang province caused by possible transnational flows of (or support for) Muslim insurgents. In fact, Pakistan has been playing a key role in actively quelling Uyghur separatist elements (such as the ETIM) on China's behalf for some years already (Yang and Siddiqi 2011: 576–577). Thus, a secondary motivation for involvement in Pakistan is to attempt to contain the Muslim separatist threat to China's northwest security outside Chinese borders as far as possible. This issue will be examined in more depth in Chapter 5.

The nature of Chinese investments constitutes another aspect of CPEC which is problematic since they are made up of loans which have to be repaid sooner or later. Used worldwide, China's "debt-based model for infrastructure development" (Jakóbowski and Kaczmarski 2017: 3) gives the impression that investment is being used as a tool to promote geopolitical interests and political influence as much as economic ones. For instance, by swapping debt for real estate, as happened with the Sri Lankan port of Hambantota in 2017 (Singh 2017), China gains long-term control over physical assets in strategic locations. China has also gained control of other ports through the more straightforward use of loan-based investments and long-term leases: this is the case in Gwadar and in Kyaukpyu in Myanmar. At any rate, the use of loans as investment instruments is suggestive of geopolitical goals being at least as important as economic ones in China's long-term strategic approach.

There are also doubts concerning the extent to which Chinese investment projects can progress smoothly and at the expected rate. Scrutiny of the official CPEC website run by the Pakistani government reveals that, as of December 2017, work had not yet begun on more than half of the 67 projects listed.[10] In these cases, individual projects are still at the planning or feasibility study stage and the timeline for substantive progress is unclear. On the other hand, China's increased pledges of cash for Pakistani energy and transport infrastructure projects in 2017 indicate firm, ongoing commitment to these two aspects of CPEC. Nonetheless, it is significant that the possibility of constructing pipelines and railways between China and Pakistan was no longer discussed in the Chinese media or other official sources from 2017 onwards. Taking on more Chinese loans – to whose repayment is invariably added compulsory insurance fees taken out with the Chinese state-backed policy insurance company Sinosure (Wolf 2020: 187–189) – to fund the building of CPEC infrastructure is a further problem which can only exacerbate the imbalance in economic relations and is likely to be the source of yet more financial problems for Pakistan in future (Venkatachalam 2017).

It might be hypothesised that China is genuinely seeking to increase economic ties with Pakistan and to boost Pakistan's economy. While this may be true, and it would seem to be in China's interest to ensure that Pakistan's economy does not completely collapse, it seems unlikely that Sino-Pakistan trade is ever going to constitute a significant proportion of China's foreign business. Pakistan's share of Chinese trade compares unfavourably with India, Vietnam, and even the Philippines (Small 2015: 96). Pakistan also has a massive trade deficit with China, importing more than six times what it exported in 2015,[11] principally because China is the main supplier of military hardware and nuclear technology to Pakistan (Ye 2009: 110). The fact that China's GDP per capita was lower than Pakistan's in 1968, but in 2012 was five times higher, further illustrates the growing gulf in economic potency between the partners (Small 2015: 95). The evidence therefore suggests that there is limited potential for Pakistan to become a major trade partner for China and that attempting the Sisyphean task of transforming it into one is not likely to be China's main goal in promoting CPEC cooperation. Pakistan's weakness and dependency also play into Chinese hands in geopolitical terms, once the strategy of geopositional hedging is taken into account. A dependent, needy Pakistan is, in fact, an ideal ally for a China intending to expand its geopolitical interests and hedge geopositionally against future conflicts with its most significant regional rival, India.

Finally, China's position regarding the potential for growth in Sino-Pakistani trade and economic interactions is summed up by an anonymous Chinese senior specialist on South Asia interviewed by Mathieu Duchâtel:

> Pakistan is a minor market for China. Economic and trade issues have only a marginal influence on the relationship.
>
> (Duchâtel 2011: 557)

In other words, geopolitical considerations are paramount for China vis-à-vis Pakistan, and economic diplomacy is mainly used as a tool to achieve the goal of bolstering China's position with regard to India in the IOR.

Pakistan's motivations for encouraging Chinese involvement in Gwadar, and for promoting CPEC generally, can be listed as follows. Above all, there is the desire to continue what it regards as a key partnership which enables it to resist pressure from its historical enemy, India (Boni 2016: 500; Aamir 2020). Pakistani military strategists keenly recall the December 1971 war with India, when the Indian navy inflicted massive damage on the Pakistani navy in Karachi port in two attacks (Ali 1983: 95). Second, the present government believes it can score points with the electorate by cultivating a Chinese business presence. Third, Pakistan is desperately short of hard currency, so seeks to obtain funds and assistance from China. And fourth, Pakistan's energy infrastructure needs an overhaul, so Chinese expertise and investment in this area are welcome. All these factors mean that Pakistan's government is generally enthusiastic about its Chinese connection, even if not all the promised investment materialises.

Overall, then, China's engagement in Pakistan at present suits both parties and in particular serves China's geopolitical interests. China gets away with maintaining the partnership through loans which have to be repaid either in cash or in equity in the projects constructed by Chinese firms (which thereby benefit), and Chinese strategists see the investment as worthwhile in order to establish a position of 'active defence' in the IOR and South Asia. Essentially, China views Pakistan principally as a counter in a larger geopolitical game aimed at geopositionally hedging against other actors in the region such as India and the United States and against possible future risk, such as a blockade of the nearby Strait of Hormuz. A secondary aim is to ensure that support in Pakistan for Uyghur separatism in Xinjiang, which could threaten China's internal security, is contained through cooperation with the Pakistani army and government. Economic factors, the 'face value' aspect of CPEC, are therefore far less significant than geopolitical and security issues.

4.6 Conclusion: geopolitics, not 'Malacca dilemma'

The evidence presented in this chapter suggests that China's intentions with CPEC are primarily geopolitical rather than geo-economic. Geographical difficulties, cost calculations, and security problems make further development of the overland connection between China and Pakistan unrealistic and unattractive, particularly with regard to the construction of oil and natural gas pipelines. Rather than taking the stated geo-economic objectives and the Malacca dilemma at face value, viewing CPEC through a geographically focused lens which evaluates Chinese motivations in terms of geopositional hedging presents a clearer picture of what China's activity in Gwadar is primarily intended to accomplish. Hedging against the regional rival India by establishing territorial footholds on the IOR littoral can be seen as China's paramount goal, with the rather fanciful notion of economically cost-effective and security-enhancing (rather than insecure) overland corridors fading into the background as geographical and geo-economic realities have dawned on Chinese policymakers.

The comparison between the proposed CPEC pipelines and completed Myanmar ones is also instructive. Despite claims to the contrary, Chinese investment in the Myanmar pipeline project has not proved to be particularly profitable nor to have significantly enhanced China's energy security. Since the empirical evidence reviewed indicates that building pipelines across Pakistan would meet with far more problems, ranging from security issues to geographical difficulties to irrational amounts of money spent on construction and maintenance, it is highly likely that this part of the CPEC project has already been quietly shelved. Indeed, in 2017 official Chinese sources continued to emphasise investment in Pakistani energy projects while mention of pipelines and the overland connection to Xinjiang was conspicuously absent from published material.

Yet the Chinese interest in the port of Gwadar remains, even though the port has not been developed much since Phase I was completed in 2007. This chapter's argument is that the Chinese interest in Gwadar, and other IOR ports such as Kyaukpyu in Myanmar and Hambantota in Sri Lanka, is primarily due to the strategy of geopositional hedging with regard to India and, to an extent, the United States. Converting debt to equity, as China did in Sri Lanka by acquiring a 70 per cent stake in Hambantota Port (Singh 2017), gives China a maritime presence which it had previously lacked. In this interpretation, CPEC is more about bolstering China's position in Pakistan than about economic cooperation, although, in fact, security goals can be achieved alongside economic ones because commercial "facilities could be quickly flipped for military application" (Drun 2017).

In the end, the reality of China's involvement in Pakistan consists mainly of efforts to sustain the geopositional footholds in the IOR gained so far as an insurance policy against as-yet-unknown future eventualities, rather than being the tale of large-scale geo-economic expansion that is told by some over-optimistic commentators. In essence, as geopolitical realities confront impractical pipeline fantasies, CPEC is, for the most part, the acceptable face of China's attempt at establishing a geopositional balancing act in the Indian Ocean. The evidence outlined in this chapter suggests that the overland connection is beset with difficulties because of geographical, economic and security problems. Indeed, there is little evidence of enthusiasm for a cross-border pipeline on the Chinese side.

Instead, China's motivation for maintaining a presence in Pakistan is likely to be chiefly geopolitical rather than geo-economic. As far as the Chinese are concerned, involvement in Gwadar is part of a long-term policy of establishing bases in the Indian Ocean in support of the Maritime Silk Road, a strategy which has been called the 'string of pearls' but which is here instead referred to as geopositional hedging.

Notes

1 This chapter is adapted from Garlick (2018).
2 Gwadar Port Authority website, 'Port Profile: Current Port Infrastructure'. Available at: www.gwadarport.gov.pk/portprofile.aspx (accessed 28 February 2021).
3 Official CPEC website. Available at: http://cpec.gov.pk/project-details/35 (accessed 7 February 2017).
4 Gwadar Port Authority website, Port Profile: Current Port Infrastructure. Available at: www.gwadarport.gov.pk/portprofile.aspx (accessed 2 March 2021).
5 According to information on ship sizes obtained from Maritime Connector website. Available at: http://maritime-connector.com/wiki/ship-sizes/ (accessed 7 February 2017).
6 Official CPEC website, Available at: http://cpec.gov.pk/project-details/35 (accessed 4 December 2017).
7 Hofstra University website Available at: https://people.hofstra.edu/geotrans/eng/ch5en/appl5en/tankers.html (accessed 7 February 2017).
8 Official CPEC website, 'Progress update'. Available at: http://cpec.gov.pk/progress-update (accessed 4 December 2017).
9 See China's Defence White Paper: *China's Military Strategy*, The State Council Information Office of the People's Republic of China, Beijing, May 2015, Section III. Full English text Available at: www.chinadaily.com.cn/china/2015-05/26/content_20820628.htm (accessed 22 March 2017).
10 Official CPEC website, 'Progress update'. Available at: http://cpec.gov.pk/progress-update (accessed 4 December 2017).
11 National Bureau of Statistics of China, *China Statistical Yearbook 2016*, Section 11–6, 'Value of Imports and Exports by Country (Region) of Origin/Destination'.

References

Aamir, Adnan (2020) 'China and Pakistan Ink Military MOU to Counter US-India Pact', *Nikkei Asian Review*, 8 December. Available at: https://asia.nikkei.com/Politics/International-relations/China-and-Pakistan-ink-military-MOU-to-counter-US-India-pact (accessed 27 February 2021).

Ali, Tariq (1983) *Can Pakistan Survive? The Death of a State*, New York: Penguin.

Amirthan, Shawn (2016) 'What Are India, Iran, and Afghanistan's Benefits from the Chabahar Port Agreement?' *Strategic Analysis*, Vol. 41, No. 1, pp. 87–93.

Aneez, Shihar, and Ranga Sirilal (2017) 'Sri Lanka Rejects Chinese Request for Submarine Visit: Sources', *Reuters*, 11 May. Available at: www.reuters.com/article/us-sri-lanka-china-submarine/sri-lanka-rejects-chinese-request-for-submarine-visit-sources-idUSKBN1871P9 (accessed 29 September 2017).

Bagchi, Indrana (2016) 'Dhaka Cancels Port to Be Built by China, India Eyes Another', *Times of India*, 8 February. Available at: http://timesofindia.indiatimes.

com/india/Dhaka-cancels-port-to-be-built-by-China-India-eyes-another/articleshow/50894554.cms (accessed 28 September 2017).

Bloomberg News (2017) 'China Opens Delayed Myanmar Oil Pipeline to Get Mideast Crude Faster', 11 April. Available at: www.bloomberg.com/news/articles/2017-04-11/china-opens-delayed-myanmar-oil-link-to-get-mideast-crude-faster (accessed 18 September 2017).

Boni, Filippo (2016) 'Civil-Military Relations in Pakistan: A Case Study of Sino-Pakistani Relations and the Port of Gwadar', *Commonwealth & Comparative Politics*, Vol. 54, No. 4, pp. 498–517.

Brewster, David (2017) 'Silk Roads and Strings of Pearls: The Strategic Geography of China's New Pathways in the Indian Ocean', *Geopolitics*, Vol. 22, No. 2, pp. 269–291.

Callahan, William A. (2008) 'Chinese Visions of World Order: Post-Hegemonic or a New Hegemony?' *International Studies Review*, Vol. 10, No. 4, pp. 749–761.

Cao Siqi and Shan Jie (2017) 'Sino-Myanmar Oil Pipeline Launch a Good Signal: Experts', *Global Times*, 28 March. Available at: www.globaltimes.cn/content/1039861.shtml (accessed 18 September 2017).

Cao, Siqi and You Ma (2017) 'China, Myanmar Ink Oil Pipeline Deal', *Global Times*, 10 April. Available at: www.globaltimes.cn/content/1041785.shtml (accessed 18 September 2017).

Chan, Mya Htwe (2017) 'Myanmar Exports 2m Tonnes of Oil Via Pipeline Over 4 Months', *Myanmar Times*, 21 September. Available at: www.mmtimes.com/news/myanmar-exports-2m-tonnes-oil-pipeline-over-4-months.html (accessed 22 November 2017).

Chaziza, Mordechai (2016) 'China-Pakistan Relationship: A Game-Changer for the Middle East?' *Contemporary Review of the Middle East*, Vol. 3, No. 2, pp. 1–15.

Chen, Aizhu and Aung Hla Tun (2016) 'New China Refinery Faces Delay as Myanmar Seeks Extra Oil Tax: Sources', *Reuters*, 10 October. Available at: www.reuters.com/article/us-china-myanmar-oil-idUSKCN12A0JF (accessed 8 February 2017).

Cohen, Saul Bernard (2015) *Geopolitics: The Geography of International Relations* (3rd ed.), Lanham, MA: Rowman & Littlefield.

Dasgupta, Saibal (2017) 'China to Seal Border with Pakistan to Curb Terror', *The Times of India*, 11 January. Available at: http://timesofindia.indiatimes.com/world/china/china-to-seal-border-with-pakistan-to-curb-terror/articleshow/56468455.cms (accessed 2 April 2017).

Ding, Gang (2017) 'China, India Could Help Stabilize Myanmar's Conflict-Ridden Rakhine State', *Global Times*, 8 February. Available at: www.globaltimes.cn/content/1032014.shtml (accessed 9 February. 2017).

Drun, Jessica (2017) 'China's Maritime Ambitions: A Sinister String of Pearls or a Benevolent Silk Road (or Both)?' *Party Watch Initiative*, 5 December. Available at: www.ccpwatch.org/single-post/2017/12/05/China%E2%80%99s-Maritime-Ambitions-a-Sinister-String-of-Pearls-or-a-Benevolent-Silk-Road-or-Both (accessed 7 December 2017).

Duchâtel, Mathieu (2011) 'The Terrorist Risk and China's Policy Towards Pakistan: Strategic Reassurance and the "United Front"', *Journal of Contemporary China*, Vol. 20, No. 71, pp. 543–561.

Erickson, Andrew S., and Gabriel B. Collins (2010) 'China's Oil Security Pipe Dream: The Reality, and Strategic Consequences, of Seaborne Imports', *Naval War College Review*, Vol. 63, No. 2, pp. 89–111.

Express Tribune (2016) 'At Gwadar Port: Additional Multipurpose Berths in Offing', 10 March. Available at: https://tribune.com.pk/story/1062683/at-gwadar-port-additional-multipurpose-berths-in-offing/ (accessed 28 February 2021).

Fazl-e-Haider, Syed (2012) 'China Set to Run Gwadar Port as Singapore Quits', *Asia Times* (online version), 5 September. Available at: www.atimes.com/atimes/China_Business/NI05Cb01.html (accessed 6 February 2017).

Garlick, Jeremy (2018) 'Deconstructing the China–Pakistan Economic Corridor: Pipe Dreams Versus Geopolitical Realities', *Journal of Contemporary China*, Vol. 27, No. 112, pp. 519–533.

Garlick, Jeremy, and Radka Havlová (2020) 'China's "Belt and Road" Economic Diplomacy in the Persian Gulf: Strategic Hedging Amidst Saudi-Iranian Regional Rivalry', *Journal of Current Chinese Affairs*, Vol. 49, No. 1, pp. 82–105.

Graeber, Daniel J. Graeber (2016) 'Iran Emerges with Claim of Pakistani Pipeline Interest', *United Press International*, 4 November. Available at: www.upi.com/Iran-emerges-with-claim-of-Pakistani-pipeline-interest/2581478260003/ (accessed 7 February 2017).

Grygiel, Jakub J. (2006) *Great Powers and Geopolitical Change*, Baltimore: Johns Hopkins University Press.

Hartpence, Mathias (2011) 'The Economic Dimension of Sino-Pakistani Relations: An Overview', *Journal of Contemporary China*, Vol. 20, No. 71, pp. 581–599.

Idrees, Rao Qasim, Rohimi Shapiee, and Haniff Ahamat (2018) 'Energy Cost Saving and Economic Prospective of China Pakistan Economic Corridor', *International Journal of Energy Economics and Policy*, Vol. 8, No. 6, pp. 217–226.

Jakóbowski, Jakub, and Marcin Kaczmarski (2017) 'Beijing's Mistaken Offer: The "16+1" and China's Policy Towards the European Union', *OSW (Centre for Eastern Studies) Commentary No. 250*, 15 September. Available at: www.osw.waw.pl/sites/default/files/commentary_250_0.pdf (accessed 1 March 2021).

Jash, Amrita (2016) 'China's 21st Century Maritime Silk Road: Strategy for Security', in Sidda Goud and Manisha Mookherjee (eds.) *Sino-Indian Relations: Contemporary Perspective*, New Delhi: Allied Publishers.

Khan, S. (2020) 'Gwadar: Why Is Pakistan Fencing China's Belt and Road Port?' *Deutsche Welle*, 20 December. Available at: www.dw.com/en/gwadar-why-is-pakistan-fencing-chinas-belt-and-road-port/a-56026436 (accessed 27 February 2021).

Khattak, Daud (2017) 'New Wave of Terrorist Attacks Casts Doubt on Pakistan's Security Forces', *The Diplomat*, 15 February. Available at: http://thediplomat.com/2017/02/new-wave-of-terrorist-attacks-casts-doubt-on-pakistans-security-forces/?utm_content=bufferf0e19&utm_medium=social&utm_source=facebook.com&utm_campaign=buffer (accessed 22 March 2017).

Kissinger, Henry (2011) *On China*, London: Allen Lane.

Klasra, Kaswar (2019) 'Saudi Investment in Gwadar Oil Refinery to Boost China-Pakistan Corridor Project', *Alarabiya News*, 23 January. Available at: https://english.alarabiya.net/business/energy/2019/01/23/Saudi-investment-in-Gwadar-oil-refinery-to-boost-China-Pakistan-Corridor-project (accessed 27 February 2021).

Lanteigne, Marc (2008) 'China's Maritime Security and the "Malacca Dilemma"', *Asian Security*, Vol. 4, No. 2, pp. 143–161.

Leung, Guy C.K. (2011) 'China's Energy Security: Perception and Reality', *Energy Policy*, Vol. 39, pp. 1330–1337.

Li, Xuanmin (2016) 'Gwadar Port Benefits to China Limited', *Global Times*, 23 November. Available at: www.globaltimes.cn/content/1019840.shtml (accessed 1 March 2021).

Masood, Salman (2017) 'Chinese Couple Abducted in Pakistan Have Been Killed, Officials Say', *New York Times*, 12 June. Available at: www.nytimes.com/2017/06/12/world/asia/pakistan-chinese-couple-killed.html (accessed 1 March 2021).

Mearsheimer, John J., and Stephen M. Walt (2016) 'The Case for Offshore Balancing: A Superior U.S. Grand Strategy', *Foreign Affairs*, July/August, pp. 70–83.

Meyer, Eric (2015) 'With Oil and Gas Pipelines, China Takes a Shortcut Through Myanmar', *Forbes*, 9 February. Available at: www.forbes.com/sites/ericrmeyer/2015/02/09/oil-and-gas-china-takes-a-shortcut/#5fb8ca892d40 (accessed 2 April 2017).

Michel, Casey (2017) 'TAPI and CASA-1000 Remain in Project Purgatory', *The Diplomat*, 10 July 2017. Available at: http://thediplomat.com/2017/07/tapi-and-casa-1000-remain-in-project-purgatory/ (accessed 25 September 2017).

Mustafa, Khalid (2021) 'Pakistan Offers China Partnership in $9b PARCO Coastal Refinery', *The News*, 8 February. Available at: www.thenews.com.pk/print/786888-pakistan-offers-china-partnership-in-9b-parco-coastal-refinery (accessed 27 February 2021).

Myint, Shwee Yee Saw, and Henning Gloystein (2017) 'First Oil for Long-Awaited Myanmar Pipeline to China Delayed Again', *Reuters*, 24 March. Available at: www.reuters.com/article/myanmar-china-oil-idUSL3N1H13NV?rpc=401& (accessed 3 April 2017).

Neelakantani, Shailaja Neelakantani (2017) 'Four Chinese Warships Arrive on Shores of "All-Weather Friend" Pakistan for "Training" Mission', *Times of India*, 11 June. Available at: http://timesofindia.indiatimes.com/world/pakistan/four-chinese-warships-arrive-on-shores-of-all-weather-friend-pakistan-for-training-mission/articleshow/59093648.cms (accessed 29 September 2017).

Negi, S.S. (1991) *Himalayan Rivers, Lakes and Glaciers*, New Delhi: Indus Publishing Company.

Ó Tuathail, G. (1996) *Critical Geopolitics: The Politics of Writing Global Space*, Minneapolis: University of Minnesota Press.

Pasick, Adam (2014) 'China's Cancelled Burma Railway Is Its Latest Derailment in Southeast Asia', *Quartz*, 25 July. Available at: https://qz.com/240436/chinas-cancelled-burma-railway-is-its-latest-derailment-in-southeast-asia/ (accessed 8 February 2017).

Raza, Syed Irfan (2016) 'Eastern Route not Part of Economic Corridor, Claims NHA Chief', *Dawn*, 5 July. Available at: www.dawn.com/news/1269102 (accessed 1 March 2021).

Reuters (2017) 'CNPC Loads First Crude Oil into Myanmar-China Pipeline', 3 May. Available at: www.reuters.com/article/china-myanmar-oil/cnpc-loads-first-crude-oil-into-myanmar-china-pipeline-idUSL1N1I504H (accessed 21 September 2017).

Rifaat, Hamzah, and Tridivesh Singh Maini (2016) *The China-Pakistan Economic Corridor: Strategic Rationales, External Perspectives, and Challenges to Effective Implementation*, Visiting Fellow Working Paper, Washington, DC: The Stimson Center.

Selvey, Mike (2012) 'Pakistan Cricket Can Never Have Home Advantage in Soulless Emirates', *The Guardian*, 11 January. Available at: www.theguardian.com/sport/blog/2012/jan/11/pakistan-cricket-emirates (accessed 21 March 2017).

Shah, Saeed (2015) 'China to Build Pipeline from Iran to Pakistan', *The Wall Street Journal*, 9 April. Available at: www.wsj.com/articles/china-to-build-pipeline-from-iran-to-pakistan-1428515277 (accessed 7 February 2017).

Shaikh, Faheemullah, Qiang Ji, and Ying Fan (2016) 'Prospects of China-Pakistan Energy and Economic Corridor', *Renewable and Sustainable Energy Reviews*, Vol. 59, pp. 253–263.

Shin, Aung Shin (2013) 'Controversial Pipeline Now Fully Operational', *Myanmar Times*, 27 October. Available at: www.mmtimes.com/index.php/business/8583-controversial-pipeline-now-fully-operational.html (accessed 3 April 2017).

Singh, Swaran (2017) 'Why Is India Worried about China Consolidating in Sri Lanka?' *The Sunday Leader*, 13 August. Available at: www.thesundayleader.lk/2017/08/13/why-is-india-worried-about-china-consolidating-in-sri-lanka/ (accessed 28 September 2017).

Small, Andrew (2010) 'China's Caution on Afghanistan-Pakistan', *The Washington Quarterly*, Vol. 33, No. 3, pp. 81–97.

Small, Andrew (2015) *The China-Pakistan Axis: Asia's New Geopolitics*, Oxford: Oxford University Press.

Storey, Ian (2006) 'China's "Malacca Dilemma"', *China Brief*, Vol. 6, No. 8 (The Jamestown Foundation), 12 April. Available at: https://jamestown.org/program/chinas-malacca-dilemma/ (accessed 8 February 2017).

Usman, Maryam, and Sardar Sikander (2016) 'CPEC's Western Route to Be Ready by 2018', *The Express Tribune*, 16 June. Available at: https://tribune.com.pk/story/1123811/western-route-ready-2018-ahsan/ (accessed 22 March 2017).

Venkatachalam, K.S. (2017) 'Can Pakistan Afford CPEC?' *The Diplomat*, 16 June. Available at: https://thediplomat.com/2017/06/can-pakistan-afford-cpec/ (accessed 22 November 2017).

Willasey-Wilsey, Tim (2016) 'Gwadar and the "String of Pearls"', *Gateway House: Indian Council on Global Relations*, 28 January. Available at: www.gatewayhouse.in/gwadar-and-the-string-of-pearls-2/ (accessed 6 February 2017).

Wolf, Siegfried O. (2020) *The China-Pakistan Economic Corridor of the Belt and Road Initiative: Concept, Context and Assessment*, Cham, Switzerland: Springer.

Xinhua Economic News (2009) 'Constructions Begin on Wharf for China-Myanmar Crude Oil Pipeline', 3 November. Available on *Downstream Today* website at: http://downstreamtoday.com/news/article.aspx?a_id=19041 (accessed 8 February 2017).

Yang, Jian, and Rashid Ahmed Siddiqi (2011) 'About an "All-Weather" Relationship: Security Foundations of Sino-Pakistan Relations Since 9/11', *Journal of Contemporary China*, Vol. 20, No. 71, pp. 563–579.

Ye, Hailin (2009) 'China-Pakistan Relationship: All-Weathers, But Maybe Not All-Dimensional', in K. Zetterlund (ed.) *Pakistan – Consequences of Deteriorating Security in Afghanistan*, Stockholm: Swedish Defence Research Agency, pp. 108–130.

Yu, Yu Myint Than (2015) 'Myanmar Pipeline Brings Gas to China, Hardship to Villagers', *National Resource Governance Institute (NRGI) Website*, 5 November. Available at: www.resourcegovernance.org/blog/myanmar-pipeline-brings-gas-china-hardship-villagers (accessed 8 March 2017).

Zhao Tingyang (2006) 'Rethinking Empire from a Chinese Concept "All-Under-Heaven"' (Tian-xia, 天下), *Social Identities*, Vol. 12, No. 1, pp. 29–41.

5 CPEC's hidden face

Geopolitics and security

5.1 Introduction: security and geopolitics as drivers of CPEC

The previous chapters revealed that the 'game changer', 'Malacca dilemma', and 'economic corridor' tropes do not tell the full story of CPEC – and, in fact, are largely misleading. This chapter will take the analysis to a deeper level by examining the geopolitical and security issues underlying CPEC in more detail. Probing further into the history of China-Pakistan cooperation since the Sino-Indian War of 1962 will demonstrate that there are many reasons to believe that geopolitical and security factors – rather than economic ones – underlie the CPEC megaproject in much the same way as they formed the basis for the close relations between the two countries in the half century preceding CPEC. It is important to take into account the development of Pakistan since its foundation in 1947 and China's long-term approach to its regions bordering Pakistan and India. Although CPEC is described as an 'economic corridor' project, this chapter expands upon the argument already advanced that CPEC's economic aspects are secondary to geopolitical and security motivations for enhanced cooperation.

In essence, for both countries there are five drivers of the expansion of political and economic ties through CPEC (see Table 5.1). The first two drivers are common to the two actors, and both are related to issues of security and geopolitics. Because they are shared, they are the most important drivers since they act as the glue cementing Sino-Pakistani cooperation. The other three drivers are not shared but are still connected to the first two and are connected to questions of national security and geopolitics.

The first shared driver is China and Pakistan's tense relations with India, with which both have clashed repeatedly in border regions over the past three-quarters of a century (S. Pande 2018: 433). It suits China to have Pakistan assist in tying down large numbers of Indian troops in Kashmir, thus easing to an extent the pressure on China's border defences by spreading the load (Niazi 2005). To be sure that Pakistan can perform this role, China needs to ensure (despite Beijing's occasional protests to the contrary) that Pakistan has sufficient military capabilities to be able to keep India busy (Small 2015: 61). As far as CPEC is concerned, from China's point of view, energy and transportation infrastructure investments

DOI: 10.4324/9781003018377-5

Table 5.1 China and Pakistan's national security priorities with regard to CPEC

Pakistan's security priorities	*China's security priorities*
Countering India	Countering India
Suppressing separatist movements (Balochistan, Sindh, NWFP)	Suppressing separatist movements (Tibet, Xinjiang)
Strengthening civil-military elites' hold on governance	Geopositional hedging in the Indian Ocean region
Economic growth to build state competence and enhance national solidarity & security	'Going out': generating commercial opportunities for Chinese companies abroad
Enhanced transport and energy infrastructure increases military capabilities	Expanding political influence in BRI countries

Source: author

are necessary to enhance Pakistan's ability to fulfil its security obligations vis-à-vis India: apart from other considerations related to Pakistan's overall economy, modern armies need consistent energy supplies and good-quality roads for support purposes. At the same time, it suits Pakistan to have China's support in what its elites – which dominate Pakistan's political economy – see as a long-term existential struggle against India (Boni 2020: 4). As Syed (1974: 15) puts it, "Pakistan's relations with China have developed largely in response to her security needs."

The second shared driver of cooperation is the problems both countries have experienced in dealing with separatist elements inside their borders. For China, the most serious separatist tendencies have occurred in Xinjiang and Tibet. Both provinces are key to Beijing's long-term geopolitical and geo-economic strategies. They contain vital resources of water (China's major rivers originate in Tibet) and oil (Xinjiang). Xinjiang is also a crucial conduit for energy supplies from Central Asia (pipelines) and overland transit to Europe. In addition, Xinjiang provides China's overland route to Pakistan, while Tibet borders Indian-controlled Kashmir. Thus, Beijing views the maintenance of control over both provinces as vital to its national security in both political and economic terms. For Pakistan, there are numerous hotspots of separatist or other terrorist activity, the most notable of which are in Balochistan, Sindh, and in the northwest border region of Khyber Pakhtunkhwa (KPK): all of these are relatively distant from the centre of government in Islamabad. Most notably, Balochistan contains Gwadar port, the development of which is supposed to be a focal point of CPEC, as well as being endowed with coal mines and other natural resources: thus, suppressing separatism and fulfilling the aims of CPEC are closely interlinked in Balochistan.

This chapter presents the argument that these two shared drivers of cooperation – containing India and suppressing separatism – constitute the glue that holds China-Pakistan cooperation together. The two shared and mutually co-constituted drivers constitute the basis for continuing the cooperation initiated in the 1960s. In essence, the name 'China-Pakistan Economic Corridor' is a new label stuck on an old tin. CPEC refers to the intensification of existing cooperation (due to the addition of increased Chinese investment in Pakistani energy and transportation infrastructure), rather than an entirely new phenomenon.

Beyond the two shared drivers, the other drivers are not directly shared. However, they do contain shared elements. For Pakistan's civil-military elites, bolstering their control over the state is a security issue which affects their interests. In addition, from their point of view holding on to power is vital for sustaining the existence of the inherently fragile nation state. The goal of maintaining control of Pakistan's power structures is closely connected to the first two drivers and underlies them. Another driver for Pakistan's elites is economic growth: the elites hope that China's investment and infrastructure building capabilities will serve to increase the ability of the Pakistani state to improve the quality of life of the people and thus to enhance national solidarity and security. Again, this driver is connected to the other three in that it refers to questions of national security from the point of view of the elites' hold over the fragile Pakistani state. The final driver is that enhanced transport and energy infrastructure built by the Chinese should support the Pakistani military's capabilities to go about its business of countering India and suppressing separatist tendencies in remote provinces with previously poor infrastructure.

China's additional drivers are different from Pakistan's. First, China's government is well aware that it does not have national territory on the Indian Ocean littoral. Therefore, the Chinese ability to project power in the IOR is severely limited. For this reason, as was explained in Chapter 4, Chinese involvement in Gwadar port can be seen as a form of geopositional hedging against future risk by enhancing China's ability to project power in the IOR in the long-term – even if in the short- to medium-term Gwadar may not appear to be particularly useful or functional.

Another driver of cooperation for China is its need to find overseas markets for its construction companies. This corresponds to the 'going out' campaign which began in 1999 (Yeh and Wharton 2016); it also draws on the idea of industrial overcapacity in the domestic Chinese market forcing Chinese companies to find commercial opportunities abroad (Kenderdine and Ling 2018). Accordingly, CPEC provides business for Chinese construction companies in Pakistan, specifically in the areas of energy and transportation infrastructure. Although this driver does not appear to be directly security related, it ties into the Chinese interpretation of national security (*guojia anquan*, 国家安全) as being connected to 'comprehensive national power' (*zonghe guoli*, 综合国力), which is obtained, in part, by obtaining "economic and political advantages abroad" (Zhang 2010: 398). The funding for infrastructure investments comes from Chinese state financial institutions such as Exim Bank, leading to accusations that China is creating a 'debt trap' for Pakistan. However, some scholars have cast doubt on the notion of China's 'debt-trap diplomacy', pointing out – for instance – that investment and loans are a two-way street involving agreements signed by both partners in a bilateral deal (Singh 2020; Xu and Li 2020). Brautigam (2020) notes that 'debt-trap diplomacy' is a meme which originated from an Indian think tank in 2017. Accordingly, instead of focusing on alleged debt traps, it is probably more logical to think of Chinese loans and infrastructure packages as generating opportunities for Chinese companies, as well as – in the case of CPEC – increasing Beijing's political influence with the Pakistani civil-military elites and thus contributing to China's 'comprehensive national power'.

This brings us to the final driver of CPEC cooperation for China: sustaining and expanding political influence. Despite Beijing's repeated claims to 'non-interference' in the internal affairs of other countries, logically it is not possible to negotiate bilateral deals between heads of state and their proxies – as China has repeatedly done in many countries – without political influence being involved. For instance, attempts to exert political influence can be identified as part of the package of China's economic diplomacy in the Czech Republic (Garlick 2019a, 2019b). It goes without saying that negotiations about China's CPEC investments involve backroom discussions between Chinese and Pakistani elites. Merely by discussing investment projects at the elite level, China exerts a degree of influence in Pakistan's internal affairs by backing the interests of those elites above other Pakistani actors. Above all, the Chinese presence in Gwadar port, in restive Balochistan, constitutes involvement in the internal affairs of the province. Local protests and terrorist attacks on Chinese nationals (Jamshed and Abid 2015; Hashim 2018; Boni 2020: 67) testify to the fact that Balochs themselves consider the Chinese involvement in Gwadar a form of interference in their regional affairs.

To examine in depth the security and geopolitical aspects of China-Pakistan cooperation – of which CPEC is the most recent manifestation – we first need to understand Pakistan's historical struggles to establish and maintain itself as a state entity. It is important to understand the troubled history of the state of Pakistan to comprehend national elites' motivation for maintaining close cooperation with China: China's support helps them to maintain their tenuous grip on a fragmented nation. We also need to consider the importance of the Tibet and Xinjiang questions for the People's Republic of China's relations with neighbouring Pakistan and India since the foundation of the PRC in 1949. China needs Pakistan's support in its efforts to maintain control over these two vital but troublesome regions far from China's main population centres. We then need to connect Pakistan and China's parallel efforts to suppress separatist movements to their need to counter the Indian presence in Kashmir. Examining all these issues together reveals that there is a remarkable convergence of interests on the Pakistani and Chinese sides which gives CPEC cooperation much more of a geopolitical tint than the officially endorsed geo-economic vision promoted since around 2014–2015 would suggest.

5.2 Pakistan: a history of turmoil

As outlined in Chapter 2, Pakistan's history has, from the nation's inception in its partition from India in 1947, unfortunately not been peaceful. The various ethnic groups within the state – most prominently, Punjabis, Sindhis, Balochs, and Pashtuns – have found it difficult to get along. As a result, Pakistan's relations with its neighbours – India, China, Afghanistan, and Iran – and the wider world have at all stages been impacted by Pakistan's struggle to establish itself as a functioning state. This section will delve into the struggle of Pakistan's civil-military elites to maintain control over a potentially fracturing entity since its inception in order to draw out the implications for CPEC and China-Pakistan cooperation in general.

5.21 Partition to the present

The state of Pakistan was formed in 1947 in the partition from India orchestrated by the British. The partition resulted in huge migrations of Muslims from India into Pakistan and Hindus in the other direction. There was massive inter-religious conflict and slaughter during this migration (Ispahani 2017: 15–16). Since then, there have been four wars between India and Pakistan, usually concerning the disputed Kashmir region: in 1947–1948, 1965, 1971, and 1999. During the Zia administration (1978–1988), "[n]ational security experts began to describe Pakistan as being encircled by India since Kabul was, at the time, more closely aligned with Delhi than Islamabad" (Saeed et al 2014: 210). Thus, Pakistan's neighbourhood foreign policy has been, from its earliest days, forged in its antagonistic reaction to India (Syed 1974: 15; S. Pande 2018: 425). Arguably, so has the nation's identity.

However, there is another aspect to Pakistan's foundation story which has frequently been noted by scholars of Pakistan's history but has not been incorporated into most analyses of CPEC. Pakistan as a state has been, from its beginning, a fractious and fragile entity made up of a number of distinct ethnic groups which tend to come into conflict with each other (Talbot 1998; Noman 2009; Saeed et al 2014: 210; Ispahani 2017). In these circumstances, it is perhaps natural that one group – the Punjabis, who make up 44.7 per cent of the population (CIA World Factbook 2021) – has tended to dominate the governance of the country in a process which has been called 'Punjabisation' (Talbot 1998: 1). Pakistan's Punjabi elites, allied with the descendants of Muslim migrants from India who settled in Pakistan's major urban centres in the 1950s (Noman 2009: 20), have taken it upon themselves to hold the country together, often using Islamisation as a tool for nation-building (Pande et al 2018: 2).

Pakistan's elites are well aware that they are surrounded by numerically smaller but often restive ethnic groups such as the Sindhs, Balochis, and Pashtuns. The need to maintain the existence of the fragile nation state while protecting their own security and interests has been uppermost in the minds of these elites (Pande et al 2018: 2). The centralisation of power in their hands has allowed Pakistan to survive, but at the same time, it has generated a sense of injustice and inequality among the nation's ethnic minorities since the elites have clearly allocated an outsized proportion of resources to themselves in a process which has been called 'elite capture' (Gul 2018). As far as minorities are concerned, "[c]entrist state structures have reinforced a sense that Pakistani nationalism is being imposed from above" (Talbot 1998: 1).

In its early decades, Pakistan consisted of West and East Pakistan: East Pakistan was the original name for what is now called Bangladesh. Bangladesh, which was always a linguistically, ethnically and geographically distinct entity, earned its independence from the state of Pakistan in the bitter and bloody civil war of 1971 (Noman 2009: 47). The Bengalis were supported in this struggle by India (Pande et al 2018: 2), generating another reason for Pakistan to mistrust its larger neighbour. Bangladesh's independence meant that Pakistan lost the entire eastern half of its territory. However, instead of bringing greater unity to the surviving western half of the country, Pakistan's post-1971 history has continued to be filled with internal violence and instability as the army and elites sought to suppress further separatist tendencies amid ever-increasing terror attacks (Saeed et al 2014). Pakistan's Punjabi and associated elites are thus acutely aware of the need to ensure that more pieces of territory – such as Balochistan – are not lost to separatist movements (Pande et al 2018: 2).

Throughout its short history, Pakistan has been riven by instability and political turmoil, most notably in Balochistan (Noman 2009: 66). Several times, a budding democracy has been rudely undermined by coups d'état led by military officers. After partition and the 1947–1948 war with India, Pakistan's budding democracy underwent an immediate setback when Liaquat Ali Khan, the nation's first prime minister and one of the founding fathers of the state, was assassinated in 1951 (Talbot 1998: 139). In 1958, General Ayub Khan seized power after martial law was imposed by President Iskander Mirza (Noman 2009: 12). Rapid economic growth under Ayub Khan was disrupted by a second war with India in 1965. When Ayub Khan was forced to hand over the presidency to General Yahya Khan in 1969, the new president immediately dissolved democratic institutions and reimposed martial law (Talbot 1998: 183). Soon after, East Pakistan's 1971 struggle for independence sparked another war between India and Pakistan which India won. This outcome freed the new nation of Bangladesh of the rule of Punjabi-dominated West Pakistan, during which Bengalis had been forced to accept Urdu as their official language.

After losing Bangladesh, President Yahya Khan was promptly replaced by Zulfikar Ali Bhutto, who re-established democracy in 1972 and founded the Pakistan People's Party (PPP). A brief democratic interlude ended in 1977 with another military coup, after which General Zia-ul-Haq became president in 1978. Former President and Prime Minister Bhutto was executed by hanging in 1979 (Talbot 1998: 258). Under President Zia, Pakistan's economy grew until Zia died in a plane crash in 1988 (Talbot 1998: 284). Bhutto's daughter, Benazir Bhutto, was twice elected prime minister as Pakistan managed to re-establish democratic processes. However, after Pakistan's defeat in yet another war with India in 1999 and consequent civil-military turmoil, General Pervez Musharraf took power in a bloodless coup (Bennett Jones 2002: 34–55). He remained as president until the democratic elections of 2008, which the PPP won after Benazir Bhutto's assassination in 2007 (Boni 2020: 59). Since 2008, Pakistan has managed to sustain democracy: the current prime minister is the former international cricketer Imran Khan, who was elected as the head of the Pakistan Tehreek-e-Insaf party (PTI) in 2018. However, internal inter-ethnic violence has continued, with kidnappings, bombings, and murders still making the lives of citizens and the business environment insecure. Pakistan's internal problems and their economic impacts – most notably high levels of debt and shortage of cash reserves (see Chapter 3) – have also made it difficult to maintain stable relations with foreign states, most notably with Pakistan's two most likely benefactors, the United States and China.

In any case, the apparent stability of Pakistan's democratic institutions since 2008 may be somewhat deceptive. There is no doubt, as Siddiqa (2007) and Noman (2009) have demonstrated, that the military, as it has done throughout Pakistan's history, still holds considerable influence behind the scenes over the political and economic life of the country. As Noman (2009: 67–68) puts it, there is

> a vocabulary in Pakistani politics which favours military intervention. The army élite sees itself as a national force, which must intervene to cement and preserve a nation threatened by treacherous politicians.

Thus, the fact that Asim Saleem Bajwa, who served as the chairman of the CPEC Authority until he was replaced in August 2021, is a retired three-star general in the Pakistani army is not at all surprising. Nor are allegations that Bajwa's "family empire had grown in sync with his rise in the Pakistani military" (Inayat 2020; see also Noorani 2020 for details of the allegations), or that Prime Minister Imran Khan would choose in September 2020 to ignore such allegations and retain Bajwa as head of the CPEC authority. That Pakistan's military would aim to exert as much control as possible over the running of the Chinese-financed megaproject is logical. This arrangement also suits the Chinese, as Boni (2020: 103–104) points out:

> The high emphasis on their investments' security that the Chinese have repeatedly manifested has placed the Army at the centre stage vis-à-vis CPEC's internal security . . . and there appear to be limited prospects for the elected government to make significant gains in civilian control in this decision-making area. This is not surprising if we place CPEC into the broader framework of Sino-Pakistani relations, in which the military have constantly represented the backbone of the partnership.

Thus, a thread of institutional instability and the tendency to revert from democratic processes to military dictatorship – especially in times of crisis – runs through Pakistan's history. The secession of East Pakistan in 1971 to become Bangladesh and the continued sectarian violence within Pakistan reveal the structural weaknesses within the state. They also reveal the existential motivation for the country's Punjab-based civil-military elites to strive to maintain influence in order to hold the country together through top-down means. Allied with the weaknesses in Pakistan's economy outlined in Chapter 3, the implication is that for Pakistan's elites, CPEC – like all previous cooperation with China – has two main drivers. First, it is a means to shore up their position of control domestically. And second, it serves to sustain the joint anti-Indian effort with China. It achieves both of these goals by focusing Chinese investments on much-needed transportation and energy infrastructure, added under the oversight of Pakistan's civil-military elites. The huge increase in Chinese personnel in Pakistan working on construction projects since the advent of CPEC in 2014–2015 is one sign of the fact that Pakistan has drawn Beijing into a position where it is deeply committed to cooperation: there are now tens of thousands of Chinese living and working in Pakistan (see Figure 5.1). The Gwadar port development, although of unclear long-term utility (even if one takes account of the geopositional hedging hypothesis advanced in Chapter 4), is another sign that China is committed to building up Pakistan's capabilities. Bolstering Pakistan's ability to sustain and defend itself serves the purpose of ensuring that India is busy with more than just its border disputes with China. And, as we will see in the next few sections, the underlying security aspects of the commitment to Pakistan keep Beijing interested in CPEC despite the ongoing economic problems inherent in the megaproject's implementation.

5.22 *Terrorism in Pakistan and its implications for CPEC*

Saeed et al (2014: 209–210) suggest that Pakistan's persistent problems with terrorist violence stem from the Zia regime's fostering of Islamization in the

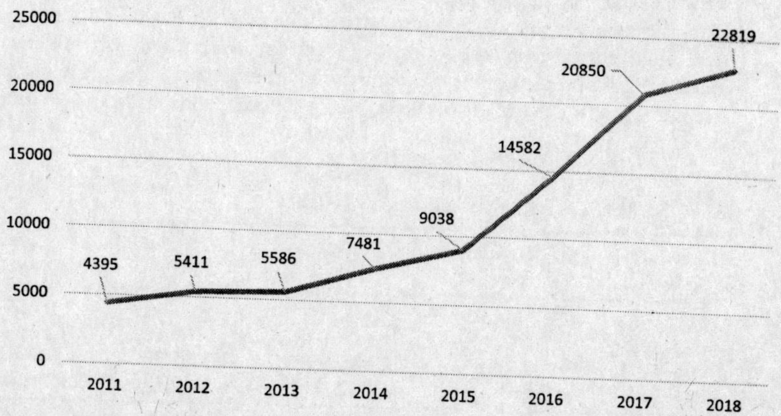

Figure 5.1 China's dispatched labour to Pakistan

Source: China Statistical Yearbook, 2012–2019 editions

1980s as an attempt to bolster regime legitimacy. According to this explanation, religious tensions increased because the Shiite minority in Pakistan became concerned about Sunni Saudi Arabia's support for Zia's Islamisation drive. Shiite Iran began to support Shiite minorities in Pakistan, engendering "a proxy terrorist war within the borders of Pakistan" (Saeed et al 2014: 210). Certainly, the data demonstrate that terrorist violence increased exponentially between 1981 and 2010: there were 26,724 casualties of terrorist violence between 2000 and 2010 compared to 1,770 between 1981 and 1989 (Saeed et al 2014: 213; see Table 4.2). A resurgence of Shia-Sunni tensions in September 2020 demonstrates that the issue of sectarian violence should not be underestimated – even if it is possible in this case that tensions were stirred up by the military and government in order to distract attention away from the negative publicity surrounding erstwhile CPEC Authority chairman retired Lieutenant General Asim Bajwa's business empire in the United States (Siddiqa 2020).

On the other hand, Shia-Sunni sectarian tensions do not tell the full story of Pakistan's troubled history of terrorist violence. Noman (2009: 66) points out that guerrilla groups in Balochistan have been resisting the central government "almost continually" since the creation of the state of Pakistan in 1947. Baloch grievances are not primarily connected to Islam, but are instead separatist in character: militant Balochs, like the Bengalis in 1971 and the Xinjiang Uyghurs of the present day, want to establish an independent state for their people and are willing to resist the central state, violently if necessary. Some Sindhis and Pashtuns have similar motivations for resistance and have similar grievances about their effective exclusion from Pakistan's political structures over the long term.

Pakistan's ethnic divisions have always affected the efforts of the nations' civil-military elite to unify the country and maintain control. In Balochistan, the situation is complicated by the fact that the Baloch population is spread out across territory which belongs to three nations: Pakistan, Iran, and Afghanistan. Similarly, there are significant Pashtun populations in both Pakistan and Afghanistan. The Sindhis occupy the territory of south-eastern Pakistan, where Karachi is located. Each of these groups seeks at the minimum greater influence in decision-making regarding the affairs of the regions which they inhabit. Militant elements

Table 5.2 Pakistan terrorism statistics, 1981–2010

Years	*Number of incidents*	*Wounded*	*Killed*	*Casualties*
1981–1989	186	1,467	303	1,770
1990–1999	1,977	4,338	2,405	6,743
2000–2010	3,264	12,997	13,727	26,724
1981–2010	5,427	18,802	16,435	35,237

Source: Saeed et al (2014: 213), based on data from the Global Terrorism Database and South Asian Terrorism Portal

in each group press for total independence from the Pakistani state, by violent means if necessary.

The state of Pakistan is thus divided between four main ethnic groups: Punjabis, Sindhis, Balochs, and Pashtuns. Six major languages are spoken, among which Urdu is used as a first language by only around 7.5 per cent of the population (Manan and David 2014: 207). Urdu and English "are used in the domains of power such as government, education, law, corporate sector, research, and media" (Manan and David 2014: 206). This means that speakers of minority languages who have not mastered Urdu or English are automatically marginalised. Since only middle-class children have access to education in Urdu or English – which according to constitutional provisions are the only two languages which can be used as official and national languages – the children of minorities and the working classes are automatically disadvantaged and excluded from Pakistan's power structures (Manan and David 2014: 207).

Noman (2009: 63–68) demonstrates that Balochs have other valid reasons for mistrusting the central government and pursuing forms of violent resistance. In the 1970s, a moderate, democratically elected Baloch provincial administration which demonstrated willingness to cooperate with the government was accused of treason and removed, eventually being replaced by military rule in 1977. The exclusion of locally endorsed political parties from Pakistan's political structure resulted in a violent backlash. This in turn fed into elite perceptions that harsh repression was necessary, generating "a self-fulfilling logic" (Noman 2009: 67) of military occupation of Balochistan and underrepresentation of Baloch interests. In Baloch eyes, their ongoing lack of ability to influence local affairs – such as the Chinese presence in Gwadar – represents total disenfranchisement from political structures.

Antagonistic relations between the Punjabi core and the Baloch, Sindhi, and Pashtun periphery have served to undermine Pakistan's democratic institutions for decades. The resentments generated in Pakistan's outlying regions have also produced an ongoing wave of terrorism, including against Chinese nationals present in Pakistan. These attacks date back to the Musharraf era, long before the announcement of CPEC. In Balochistan, the first recorded attack on a Chinese national occurred in a 2001 rocket attack on the vehicle in which a Chinese engineer was travelling (Jamshed and Abid 2015: 87–88). There was a thwarted attack on Chinese engineers in 2003. In May 2004, three Chinese engineers working on the development of Gwadar port were killed and 11 injured by a remote-controlled bomb (Jamshed and Abid 2015: 88). In October 2004, two Chinese engineers were abducted along with their Pakistani driver and guard when working on the Gomal Zam dam: the dam is located in what was then known as the North-West Frontier Province (NWFP) but is now called Khyber Pakhtunkhwa (KPK). After negotiations for their release failed, the Pakistani military executed a commando operation to free the hostages. The operation resulted in the deaths of all five kidnappers, but also one of the two hostages, while the other was injured (Jamshed and Abid 2015: 91–93). Further attacks on Chinese nationals occurred from 2005 to 2008 in various locations across Pakistan, including six more deaths (Jamshed and Abid 2015: 107).

In the CPEC era, there have been further attacks on Chinese nationals, often connected to Balochistan. One of the most notorious occurred in 2017, when two Chinese-language teachers were kidnapped in Quetta, the capital of Balochistan. The teachers were eventually killed despite efforts by the Pakistani military to rescue them (Boni 2020: 67). In August 2018, the Baloch Liberation Army (BLA) suicide-attacked a bus containing Chinese engineers in Dalbandin, Balochistan, wounding six people (Hashim 2018). In November the BLA attacked the Chinese consulate in Karachi (Boni 2019: 5–6): two policemen and the three attackers were killed, but no Chinese nationals were harmed (Hashim 2018). Such incidents reveal the intensity of local resentment towards Chinese activity under the CPEC umbrella and militants' willingness to take violent action. China is clearly dependent on the Pakistani military for the security of Chinese operations in Balochistan and elsewhere throughout Pakistan (Boni 2019). The terrorist incidents also demonstrate "how the military provides a port of call and a privileged interlocutor" for the Chinese (Boni 2020: 67).

5.3 The China-India-Pakistan triangle

This section outlines the role of Tibet and Xinjiang in Chinese calculations regarding CPEC and cooperation with Pakistan. Then it moves on to questions concerning Chinese aims in the Indian Ocean region and the role of Gwadar port and other aspects of CPEC in achieving these aims.

5.31 The role of Tibet

After the CCP won the civil war with the Kuomindang nationalists in 1949 and founded the People's Republic of China (PRC), it was of the utmost importance to ensure that the reunited country remained intact. Since the end of the imperial era in 1911, China had been internally divided by regional warlords and Japanese invasion. Having gained power over the world's fourth biggest country by area and the largest in terms of population, it was vital for the CCP was to establish and maintain control over the entire geographical area of the country. Achieving this goal meant consolidating influence in outlying regions inhabited by non-Han ethnic minorities – most notably Tibet and Xinjiang – not least because of the potential natural resources to be obtained there. Maintaining the territorial integrity of the nation remains an overriding priority for the CCP today, just as it does for Pakistan's elites.

In 1951, the Chinese government strove to establish control over Tibet via the so-called Seventeen Point Agreement. This was agreed with the 14th Dalai Lama, who was at that time both the political and spiritual leader of Buddhist Tibet. The agreement granted the Chinese sovereignty over Tibet, although the Tibetans later claimed that they were forced to sign it under duress (Grunfeld 1996: 113–114). However, the Tibetan uprising of March 1959 put an end to dreams of harmonious cohabitation in Tibet by immigrant Han Chinese and locals. Peaceful protests turned violent and were crushed by the PLA, causing the Dalai Lama to flee to India. He was granted refuge by the Indian government and has since lived in India for over six decades, fuelling Chinese suspicion of Indian intentions regarding Tibet. Tibetan guerrillas continued to struggle against the PLA after the Dalai Lama left, but more than 87,000 fighters had been "neutralised" by October 1960 (Li 2016: 309). The Tibetan Autonomous Region was established in 1965, confirming that the PRC had gained firm control and that Tibet was incorporated into the Chinese state.

The war with India in 1962 conveniently took place at precisely the same time as the Cuban Missile Crisis, neatly ensuring that the world's attention was diverted from what was happening in the Himalayas. The war was clearly connected to India's harbouring of the Dalai Lama and other Tibetan refugees. However, the desire to send a signal to India not to actively support Tibetan independence efforts was not the sole reason behind Beijing's decision to attack Indian positions along the Himalayan border. China's leaders were also concerned by incremental Indian gains in the border region through which the Indians had managed to make inroads into Chinese-held territory (Garver 2006: 87). For historical reasons related to the colonial era, agreement on the exact line of the frontier had never been established. The decision to attack was therefore motivated by the desire both to deter India from interfering in Tibet and to ensure the PRC's control over what it believed to be its rightful line of control along the border (Garver 2006: 86–87). The war achieved China's goal of persuading India that it was a potent military force which India should not underestimate, but at the cost of ensuring long-term Indian mistrust of China's intentions (Garver 2006: 124). Memories of India's bitter 1962 defeat run deep in India: Indians today still generally remain sceptical of Chinese proclamations of friendship, and the Indian government consistently refuses to participate in either the BRI or CPEC.

Even today, skirmishes between Chinese and Indian troops in various parts of the border regions break out frequently, sometimes with deadly consequences. In June 2020, the deadliest clash since 1962 resulted in the deaths of at least 20 Indian soldiers and an unknown number of Chinese troops in the mountainous Galwan Valley (Safi et al 2020). In January 2021 there was another violent encounter in the Sikkim border region during which there were reportedly injuries on both sides (Pandit 2021). China is anxious to protect its border territories in the disputed Aksai Chin area because they contain the only road connection between Xinjiang and Tibet. The road, designated China National Highway 219, was built between 1951 and 1957, before the outbreak of the war with India. The existence of this road connection, which is probably mainly used by the PLA, partly explains China's dogged insistence on maintaining control of the area.

In short: the two countries' continued attempts to establish their claims mean that the 60-year border standoff between Chinese and Indian troops is not likely to end anytime soon. This situation, allied with the Indian government's obvious mistrust of China's intentions, clearly impacts upon any and all calculations that Beijing makes about its cooperation with Pakistan – including CPEC.

5.32 The role of Xinjiang

Xinjiang is the home of the Uyghurs, a Muslim Turkic ethnic group which has inhabited the region for centuries. Xinjiang borders Pakistan and India in the south, Afghanistan, Tajikistan, Kyrgyzstan, and Kazakhstan in the west, and Russia and Mongolia in the north. The XUAR is an important source of fossil fuels since it contains China's largest reserves of oil, natural gas, and coal (Duan et al 2016). It is also a vital trade route connecting China with Central Asia and Russia – and thence on to Europe. The route was part of the ancient Silk Road and is now intrinsic to the Silk Road Economic Belt (SREB), which constitutes the overland portion of the BRI. Oil and gas pipelines from Kazakhstan and Turkmenistan transit Xinjiang as they transport energy supplies to China's eastern provinces.

Thus, the Chinese government views Xinjiang as vital to the PRC's national economic and energy security. For the CCP, allowing Uyghurs to define themselves as a separate nation which might choose to secede from the PRC is utterly unthinkable. As in Tibet, crushing separatist tendencies in the indigenous population is of the utmost importance in establishing control over a strategically vital and resource-rich part of the PRC (Bovingdon 2010: 47).

Xinjiang was absorbed into China during the Qing dynasty. However, it was only after the foundation of the PRC that China began seriously to consolidate control with the arrival of the PLA in 1949 and the formation of the XUAR in October 1955 (Bovingdon 2010: 44). Since that time, there has been a steady migration of Han Chinese into Xinjiang in search of business opportunities (Hopper and Webber 2009: 178). This has caused the demographics of the region to shift. A 1955 census revealed that 73 per cent of Xinjiang's population was Uyghur (Bovingdon 2010: 199). However, by 2000 the Uyghur proportion of the XUAR's population had dropped to 45 per cent (Hopper and Webber 2009: 178). Over the same period, the proportion of Han Chinese rose from 6.1 per cent to 40.6 per cent of the total population (Hopper and Webber 2009: 178).

The increasing presence of Han Chinese, especially in urban areas, has caused tensions with the Uyghurs, who correctly sense that they are being pushed aside in their homeland. In July 2009 there were riots in Urumqi in which Uyghurs attacked Han Chinese, and 197 people were killed, mostly ethnic Han, and 1,721 were injured (Wong 2009). Nine Uyghur rioters were executed in November 2009. In March 2014, a group of eight assailants attacked civilians with knives at Kunming railway station in southern Yunnan province: 31 people were killed and 143 injured (BBC News 2015). Four of the Uyghur attackers were shot dead by police, while the others were arrested (Tiezzi 2014). Three of the surviving attackers were later executed, while the fourth was sentenced to life imprisonment (BBC News 2015). Alongside other incidents of Uygur attacks, the 2009 riots and 2014 Kunming knife attack shocked the Han Chinese public and caused the Chinese government to harden its approach to the Uyghurs.

The most well-known Uyghur separatist group is the East Turkestan Islamic Movement. The United Nations (UN) Security Council – of which China is a permanent member – has officially listed ETIM as a terrorist organisation linked to Al-Qaida since 2002 (UN Security Council 2011). The UN Security Council's official declaration on ETIM includes the following explanation of ETIM's activities:

> ETIM is currently active in South Asia, Central Asia and the *Xinjiang* Uygur Autonomous Region of China. . . . In recent years, ETIM has set up bases outside China to train terrorists and has dispatched its members to China to plot and execute terrorist acts including bombing buses, cinemas, department stores, markets and hotels. ETIM has also undertaken assassinations and arson attacks and has carried out terrorist attacks against Chinese targets abroad. Among the violent acts committed by ETIM members were the blowing up of the warehouse of the Urumqi Train Station on 23 May 1998, the armed looting of 247,000 RMB Yuan in Urumqi on 4 February 1999, an explosion in Hetian City, Xinjiang, on 25 March 1999 and violent resistance against arrest in Xinhe County, Xinjiang, on 18 June 1999. These incidents resulted in the deaths of 140 people and injuries to 371.
>
> (UN Security Council 2011)

The Chinese government has worked hard to crush ETIM both inside and outside the PRC. In the Muslim countries which border Xinjiang, such as Kazakhstan, Afghanistan, and Pakistan, the aim has been to ensure that the effectivity of any potential ETIM support bases is reduced as close to zero as possible. This aim appears to have been achieved, since ETIM now seems to have a vastly reduced impact on affairs in Xinjiang. Indeed, the separatist organisation appears to have been virtually wiped out, leading to the US government removing ETIM from its list of terrorist organisations in October 2020 on the basis that "for more than a decade, there has been no credible evidence that ETIM continues to exist" (Lipes 2020). Other organised Uyghur resistance movements thus far do not appear to be in evidence, indicating that the Chinese strategy has broadly succeeded in its aim of suppressing Uyghur separatism. In Pakistan, the Chinese have managed to ensure that support for the Uyghurs has not been available by coordinating anti-separatist policy behind the scenes with the Pakistani army and government.

Over the last decade, the Chinese policy of crushing resistance in Xinjiang has become increasingly controversial outside China. The Chinese government's suppression of the Uyghurs is seen as a coordinated programme of human rights abuse: some scholars and activists – and even US Secretary of State Mike Pompeo – have labelled the Chinese approach genocide (Smith Finley 2020; Bellinger 2021). In 2018, the Chinese government acknowledged the existence of 're-education camps', even revising legislation to provide official endorsement for their continued use (Gan and Lau 2018). Some have compared the Xinjiang 're-education camps' to concentration camps, albeit far less brutal versions than their twentieth-century predecessors (Roberts 2018: 251; Smith Finley 2019: 7). Up to 2 million Uyghurs are said to have been interned in these camps, although the figure is difficult to confirm. Families are said to have been split apart. There have been reports of physical and psychological abuse of prisoners in the international media (Yeung et al 2021).

As far as CPEC is concerned, the suppression of Uyghur separatism in neighbouring Xinjiang constitutes a significant factor in the Chinese commitment to Pakistan. Both Pakistan and China need to suppress separatist movements. Suppression of separatism is a common goal of both the Chinese and Pakistani states and militaries, just as they share the goal of countering the Indian presence on their border. Since CPEC is framed as an overland link between Pakistan's Gilgit-Baltistan administrative territory – which is the northern section of the Kashmir region disputed with India – and China's XUAR, it has obvious relevance to both countries' security and geopolitical goals. The fact that CPEC's overland connection passes through border territory disputed with India, containing possibly restive locals, demands incorporating careful calculations concerning India and the need to suppress separatist tendencies.

If nothing else, CPEC is a symbol of the Chinese commitment to Pakistan and Pakistan's commitment to cooperation with China. China thus expects that Pakistan would consistently oppose – or at least stay silent about – separatist movements in Xinjiang or Tibet. In accepting Chinese investment under the umbrella of CPEC, Pakistan concurs in not supporting the Uyghurs and not allowing them to establish a supply chain on the Pakistani side of the border. Even if Pakistan may not participate in any form of concerted anti-Uyghur action, it tacitly consents to non-criticism of the Chinese approach. Apart from its other aims, CPEC constitutes an important prop in China's campaign against Uyghur separatism by contributing to discouragement of any thought of support for the East Turkestan movement by the Pakistanis even though the Uyghurs, like most Pakistanis, are Muslims.

5.33 *The role of the Indian Ocean*

The Chinese involvement in Gwadar port is controversial for India. Gwadar is just one in a series of Indian Ocean ports in which Chinese companies have made investments. Others include Hambantota and Colombo in Sri Lanka, Kyaukpyu in Myanmar, Duqm in Oman, and Doraleh in Djibouti. In 2005, the US agency Booz Allen Hamilton coined the term 'string of pearls' to designate China's purported attempts to expand its naval presence in the IOR through the construction of commercial port infrastructure on the Indian Ocean littoral (Baker 2015). The term is disputed by the Chinese, but nevertheless conveys an image of Chinese expansionism which is alarming to India.

From Beijing's point of view, there is a need to beef up the Chinese presence in the IOR to protect vital SLOCs through which pass most of China's imported oil as well as other imports of raw materials (Shinn 2008: 181–182). Vital oil supplies from the Persian Gulf pass through the Strait of Hormuz: after passing through, oil tankers pass Pakistan and India on their way to the Straits of Malacca, the South China Sea, and China's eastern seaboard. Container ships carrying manufactured goods also pass through the

Indian Ocean on their way to Europe and Africa, as do vessels carrying fossil fuels and raw materials for industrial production from African countries such as Zambia (copper), Angola (oil), and Sudan (oil). However, as far as the Indian government is concerned, the increased Chinese presence constitutes a potential security threat in what it considers its IOR backyard. If the Chinese presence continues to increase, India worries that the PLAN will try to dominate the Indian Ocean.

Since 2016, India has been developing the Iranian port of Chabahar, just 70 kilometres from Gwadar by sea. The port is supposed to represent a gateway for India's trade with Afghanistan and Central Asia, bypassing Pakistan. India's reported US$500 million investment represented the nation's first foreign port venture and a clear challenge to China's Gwadar port development (Hellenic Shipping News 2021). Iran handed the port over to India in December 2018 based on an agreement signed in 2015 (Laskar 2018). However, port operations were hobbled by the restrictions the Trump administration placed on trade with Iran. The port handled only 123 vessels with 1.8 million tonnes of cargo from February 2019 to January 2021 (Hellenic Shipping News 2021). On the other hand, these figures do not look so bad in comparison with those available for Gwadar: between 2013 and 2018, only 99 vessels conveying cargo of 1.439 million tonnes docked in Gwadar (Bahadur 2018). With hopes for a resumption of the Iran nuclear deal or Joint Comprehensive Plan of Action (JCPOA) emerging under the newly installed Biden administration, India accelerated construction work: the port was due to commence full-scale operations by the end of May 2021 (Hellenic Shipping News 2021). Nevertheless, it remains to be seen whether the supposed contest between Gwadar and Chabahar to be a maritime hub for overland connections to Central Asia turns out to be anything more than a war of words.

Such calculations for China were compounded by the addition of both India and Pakistan to the Shanghai Cooperation Organization (SCO) in 2017. Founded in 2001 as a mechanism primarily to coordinate cooperation on security between Russia, China, and the Central Asian states of Kazakhstan, Kyrgyzstan, Tajikistan, and Uzbekistan (Turkmenistan, Afghanistan, and Iran are not members, but regularly attend meetings), the SCO has had a high degree of success in stabilising the Central Asian region. Possible rivalry between Russia and China for influence has been dampened and conflicts between the Central Asian states over borders minimised. In addition, through security coordination in the SCO Beijing has managed to ensure that there is zero official support among the leaders of the Muslim Central Asian states for Uyghur separatism in Xinjiang province. However, the inclusion of Pakistan and India as full members adds an extra layer of security dilemma to the SCO equation given the two countries' enmity and the Chinese favouring of Pakistan. It is not yet clear if dialogues within the SCO framework can smooth over the tensions inherent in the India-Pakistan-China triangular relationship or clarify how South Asia and the Indian Ocean will or will not be connected to Central Asia via new infrastructure, for instance as part of the BRI or CPEC.

China's attempts to gain influence in Iran constitute another aspect of the competition between China and India to develop Gwadar and Chabahar. China and Iran announced a US$400 billion trade and investment deal in March 2021 (Fassihi and Myers 2021), which, if realised, would represent a massive blow to India's hopes of exerting greater influence in Iran. However, Scita (2020) points out that similar deals have been announced several times previously with rather limited results:

> Since 2016, both the Chinese and Iranian discourse about the CSP has been dominated by big announcements and constant references to the long-lasting friendship existing between the two countries. However, the excitement periodically emerging around the partnership has rarely been matched by its actual implementation.

Indeed, the same US$400 billion deal was also announced in July 2020 (Afrasaiabi 2020) and September 2019 (Cohen 2019). On both occasions, there was very little real activity to match the publicity. Progress on the implementation of Chinese investments in Iran continues to be slow, with – as Garlick and Havlová (2020b) demonstrate – lower levels of investment than would be expected given the loud public announcements. The contest between India and China to beat out the other for influence in Iran looks set to continue as a geo-economic – or geopolitical – counterpoint to the dominant Chinese influence in neighbouring Pakistan.

In addition, the Chinese government is very much aware that it has other geopolitical factors to consider as it aims to secure energy supplies and trade routes while seeking to avoid becoming enmeshed in regional political rivalries and military conflicts. The two dominant regional powers in the Persian Gulf are Iran and Saudi Arabia, and they are bitterly opposed to each other. This rivalry manifests in proxy wars such as those in Yemen and Syria, in each of which Shiite Iran and Sunni Saudi Arabia are backing opposing factions. The problem for Beijing is that both Iran and Saudi Arabia are important suppliers of oil for China's ever-growing economy. The Chinese therefore attempt to strategically hedge their bets by cultivating relations with both rivals without antagonising either (Garlick and Havlová 2020a).

Beijing also needs to be careful not to stir up antagonistic reactions from the US, which since the Islamic revolution of 1979 has backed Saudi Arabia against Iran and will likely continue to do so. Despite evidence that US global power is gradually ebbing, the Americans retain the world's – and the region's – most powerful military. The US military occupied neighbouring Afghanistan after invading the country in October 2001 in the wake of the 9/11 attack in New York. Even though the Biden administration withdrew the last US troops from Afghanistan before the end of August 2021, there is little doubt that the United States will remain a significant military influence in the region and a major factor in Beijing and Islamabad's calculations concerning the ongoing cooperation between their countries. The US naval base in Diego Garcia in the centre of the Indian Ocean stands as a reminder to all of America's continuing ability to project power in the IOR. This, allied with China's need to protect vital shipping routes, explains China's development of IOR ports such as those in Hambantota and Colombo in Sri Lanka, Kyaukpyu in Myanmar, Doraleh in Djibouti, Duqm in Oman – and Gwadar in Pakistan.

China's need to maintain a delicate balancing act in the Persian Gulf adds to the complexity of the Chinese government's geopolitical calculations concerning neighbouring Pakistan and India. It also presents an important long-term motivation for continuing to develop and maintain a presence in the port of Gwadar. Even if the commercial potential of the port is not clear at this stage, and the potential for a land corridor from Gwadar to Kashgar is doubtful (see Chapter 4), Beijing is surely calculating that it may be useful to have a foothold in a strategic location on the Indian Ocean littoral not too far from the vital Strait of Hormuz through which a large proportion of China's oil supplies pass. Despite Chinese protestations to the contrary, Gwadar thus has a geopolitical aspect which explains China's continuing presence at the port despite the slow progress in developing the port as a commercial entity – even if the PLAN is not yet officially present in the port.

5.4 Conclusion: reconfiguring CPEC

This chapter has outlined the importance of security and geopolitical factors as drivers of cooperation between China and Pakistan. The analysis outlined earlier explains CPEC in terms of security and geopolitics rather than the economic factors usually presented as drivers. The analysis reveals that questions related to Pakistan's history of violence and instability arising from the troubled formation of the state in the partition from India in 1947 have affected its relations with India, China, and other actors. CPEC therefore needs to be understood in relation to that history rather than as a new phenomenon with purely economic motivations.

Most importantly, it needs to be acknowledged that the CPEC megaproject depends, above all, upon cooperation between Chinese and Pakistan military elites. China depends upon the Pakistani military and its proxies for the security of Chinese investments in Pakistan under the CPEC label. The head of the CPEC authority until August 2021 was a retired general in the Pakistani army with close links to the civil-military elites in Punjab who run Pakistan. Since Sino-Pakistani cooperation is, to a great extent, based on the perceived need for both partners to (1) counter India across contested borders in Kashmir and (2) to ensure security in certain troubled outlying regions of each country – Xinjiang and Tibet in the case of China, and Balochistan, Khyber Pakhtunkhwa, and Sindh in the case of Pakistan – cooperation between the Chinese and Pakistani armies on CPEC has been a given since the megaproject's inception.

The existence of CPEC can thus only be fully understood in connection with the geopolitical and security aspects of Sino-Pakistani cooperation since the 1960s relating to India and internal separatism in each partner country. The insistence or assumption in much of the CPEC literature – whether Pakistani or Chinese in origin – that CPEC has purely or mainly economic drivers and outcomes is therefore misleading and stands in need of correction – a task which this chapter and this book have attempted. Ultimately, there can be no question that the security and geopolitical aspects prevalent in the history of China's cooperation with Pakistan dominate the relations between the two countries – and also, therefore, the inception and development of the CPEC megaproject.

References

Afrasaiabi, Kaveh (2020) 'China, Iran Deal Eyes a Future Decoupled from US', *Asia Times*, 10 July. Available at: https://asiatimes.com/2020/07/china-iran-deal-eyes-a-future-decoupled-from-us/ (accessed 31 July 2020).

Bahadur, Irfan (2018) '99 Ships with 1.439 Million Ton Cargo Unloaded at Gwadar Port', *Customs Today*, 4 September. Available at: https://customstoday.com.pk/99-ships-loaded-with-1-439-million-ton-cargo-unloaded-at-gwadar-port/ (accessed 23 February 2021).

Baker, Benjamin David (2015) 'Where Is the "String of Pearls" in 2015?' *The Diplomat*, 5 October. Available at: https://thediplomat.com/2015/10/where-is-the-string-of-pearls-in-2015/ (accessed 10 April 2021).

BBC News (2015) 'China Executes Three Over Kunming Station Attack', 24 March. Available at: www.bbc.com/news/world-asia-china-32029430 (accessed 15 April 2021).

Bellinger, John B. (2021) 'China's Abuse of the Uighurs: Does the Genocide Label Fit?' *Council on Foreign Relations*, 3 February. Available at: www.cfr.org/article/chinas-abuse-uighurs-does-genocide-label-fit (accessed 16 April 2021).

Bennett Jones, Owen (2002) *Pakistan: Eye of the Storm*, New Haven and London: Yale University Press.

Boni, Filippo (2019) 'Protecting the Belt and Road Initiative: China's Cooperation with Pakistan to Secure CPEC', *Asia Policy*, Vol. 14, No. 2, pp. 5–12.

Boni, Filippo (2020) *Sino-Pakistani Relations: Politics, Military and Regional Dynamics*, Abingdon, UK: Routledge.

Bovingdon, Gardner (2010) *The Uyghurs: Strangers in Their Own Land*, New York: Columbia University Press.

Brautigam, Deborah (2020) 'A Critical Look at Chinese 'Debt-Trap Diplomacy': The Rise of a Meme', *Area Development and Policy*, Vol. 5, No. 1, pp. 1–14.

CIA World Factbook (2021) 'Pakistan', 13 April. Available at: www.cia.gov/the-world-factbook/countries/pakistan/ (accessed 16 April 2021).

Cohen, Ariel (2019) 'China's Giant $400 Billion Iran Investment Complicates U.S. Options', *Forbes*, 19 September. Available at: www.forbes.com/sites/arielcohen/2019/09/19/chinas-giant-400-billion-iran-investment-snubs-trump/#1ba5e7184d1e (accessed 27 July 2020).

Duan, Jinhui, Ming Zeng, Yanfang Ju, and Shuying Wei (2016) 'The Energy Industry in Xinjiang, China: Potential, Problems, and Solutions', *Power*, 1 January. Available at: www.powermag.com/energy-industry-xinjiang-china-potential-problems-solutions-web/ (accessed 14 April 2021).

Fassihi, Farnaz, and Steven Lee Myers (2021) 'China, with $400 Billion Iran Deal, Could Deepen Influence in Mideast', *New York Times*, 27 March. Available at: www.

nytimes.com/2021/03/27/world/middleeast/china-iran-deal.html (accessed 1 May 2021).

Gan, Nectar, and Mimi Lau (2018) 'China Changes Law to Recognise "Re-Education Camps" in Xinjiang', *South China Morning Post*, 10 October. Available at: www.scmp.com/news/china/politics/article/2167893/china-legalises-use-re-education-camps-religious-extremists (accessed 16 April 2021).

Garlick, Jeremy (2019a) 'China's Economic Diplomacy in Central and Eastern Europe: A Case of Offensive Mercantilism?' *Europe-Asia Studies*, Vol. 71, No. 8, pp. 1390–1414.

Garlick, Jeremy (2019b) 'China's Principal-Agent Problem in the Czech Republic: The Curious Case of CEFC', *Asia Europe Journal*, Vol. 17, No. 4, pp. 437–451.

Garlick, Jeremy, and Radka Havlová (2020a) 'China's "Belt and Road" Economic Diplomacy in the Persian Gulf: Strategic Hedging Amidst Saudi-Iranian Regional Rivalry', *Journal of Current Chinese Affairs*, Vol. 49, No. 1, pp. 82–105.

Garlick, Jeremy, and Radka Havlová (2020b) 'The Dragon Dithers: Assessing the Cautious Implementation of China's Belt and Road Initiative in Iran', *Eurasian Geography and Economics*. Doi: 10.1080/15387216.2020.1822197.

Garver, John W. (2006) 'China's Decision for War with India in 1962', in Alastair Iain Johnston and Robert S. Ross (eds.) *New Directions in the Study of China's Foreign Policy*, Stanford: Stanford University Press, pp. 86–130.

Grunfeld, A. Tom (1996) *The Making of Modern Tibet* (revised ed.), Armonk, NY: M.E. Sharpe.

Gul, Imtiaz (2018) 'Pakistan's Elite Capture and the State of Insecurity', in Aparna Pande (ed.) *Routledge Handbook of Contemporary Pakistan*, Abingdon, UK: Routledge, pp. 189–205.

Hashim, Asad (2018) 'Gunmen Attack Chinese Consulate in Karachi', *Al Jazeera*, 23 November. Available at: www.aljazeera.com/news/2018/11/23/gunmen-attack-chinese-consulate-in-karachi (accessed 1 May 2021).

Hellenic Shipping News (2021) 'India Doubling Down on Chabahar Port Project as Strategic Counter to China BRI Gains Momentum', 7 April. Available at: www.hellenicshippingnews.com/india-doubling-down-on-chabahar-port-project-as-strategic-counter-to-china-bri-gains-momentum/ (accessed 1 May 2021).

Hopper, Ben, and Michael Webber (2009) 'Migration, Modernisation and Ethnic Estrangement: Uygur Migration to Urumqi, Xinjiang Uyghur Autonomous Region, PRC', *Inner Asia*, Vol. 11, No. 2, pp. 173–203.

Inayat, Naila (2020) 'Asim Bajwa's Dirty Money Is RAW Saazish in Imran Khan's Pakistan', *The Print*, 10 September. Available at: https://theprint.in/opinion/letter-from-pakistan/asim-bajwas-dirty-money-is-raw-saazish-in-imran-khans-pakistan/499389/ (accessed 30 April 2021).

Ispahani, Farahnaz (2017) *Purifying the Land of the Pure: A History of Pakistan's Religious Minorities*, New York: Oxford University Press.

Jamshed, Unsa, and Massarrat Abid (2015) 'Terrorism and Sino-Pak Relationship: A Case Study of Chinese Nationals as Victims of Terrorism in Pakistan During Musharraf Regime', *Pakistan Vision*, Vol. 16, No. 2, pp. 87–116.

Kenderdine, Tristan, and Han Ling (2018) 'International Capacity Cooperation – Financing China's Export of Industrial Overcapacity', *Global Policy*, Vol. 9, No. 1, pp. 41–52.

Laskar, Rezaul H. (2018) 'India Takes Over Operations of Iran's Strategic Chabahar Port, Can Bypass Pak on Way to Afghanistan', *Hindustan Times*, 24 December.

Available at: www.hindustantimes.com/india-news/india-takes-over-chabahar-port-operations-from-iran-will-ship-supplies-to-afghanistan/story-kWKZeStt1MfQR4s5Voz4fL.html (accessed 1 May 2021).

Li, Jianglin (2016) *Tibet in Agony: Lhasa 1959*, Cambridge, MA: Harvard University Press.

Lipes, Joshua (2020) 'US Drops ETIM from Terror List, Weakening China's Pretext for Xinjiang Crackdown', *Radio Free Asia*, 5 November. Available at: www.rfa.org/english/news/uyghur/etim-11052020155816.html (accessed 16 April 2021).

Manan, Syed Abdul, and Maya Khemlani David (2014) 'Mapping Ecologies of Literacy in Educational Setting: The Case of Local Mother Tongues Vis-à-Vis Urdu and English Languages in Pakistan', *Language and Education*, Vol. 28, No. 3, pp. 203–222.

Niazi, Tarique (2005) 'China's March on South Asia', *China Brief*, Vol. 5, No. 9. Available at: https://jamestown.org/program/chinas-march-on-south-asia/ (accessed 10 April 2021).

Noman, Omar (2009) *Pakistan: Political and Economic History Since 1947*, Abingdon, UK: Routledge.

Noorani, Ahmad (2020) 'Asim Declared on Oath His Wife Has No "Business Capital Outside Pakistan"', *Fact Focus*, 27 August. Available at: https://factfocus.com/politics/1756/ (accessed 30 April 2021).

Pande, Savita (2018) 'India as a Factor in Pakistan's Policy', in Aparna Pande (ed.) *Routledge Handbook of Contemporary Pakistan*, Abingdon, UK: Routledge, pp. 425–441.

Pande, Savita, Shefali Dhar, and Sidhanta Mehra (2018) 'Introduction', In Aparna Pande (ed.) *Routledge Handbook of Contemporary Pakistan*, Abingdon, UK: Routledge, pp. 1–12.

Pandit, Rajat (2021) 'Indian, PLA Soldiers Clashed in North Sikkim on January 20: Army', *The Times of India*, 26 January. Available at: https://timesofindia.indiatimes.com/india/indian-chinese-soldiers-injured-in-physical-brawl-near-naku-la-in-sikkim/articleshow/80445589.cms (accessed 10 April 2021).

Roberts, Sean R. (2018) 'The Biopolitics of China's "War on Terror" and the Exclusion of the Uyghurs', *Critical Asian Studies*, Vol. 50, No. 2, pp. 232–258.

Saeed, Luqman, Shabib Haider Syed, and Roger P. Martin (2014) 'Historical Patterns of Terrorism in Pakistan', *Defense & Security Analysis*, Vol. 30, No. 3, pp. 209–229.

Safi, Michael, Hannah Ellis-Petersen, and Helen Davidson (2020) 'Soldiers Fell to Their Deaths as India and China's Troops Fought with Rocks', *The Guardian*, 17 June. Available at: www.theguardian.com/world/2020/jun/17/shock-and-anger-in-india-after-worst-attack-on-china-border-in-decades (accessed 10 April 2021).

Scita, Jacopo (2020) 'To Understand the China-Iran Deal, Forget the Hype and Look at the Context', *Responsible Statecraft*, 15 July. Available at: https://responsiblestatecraft.org/2020/07/15/to-understand-the-china-iran-deal-forget-the-hype-and-look-at-the-context/ (accessed 27 July 2020).

Shinn, David H. (2008) 'Military and Security Relations: China, Africa, and the Rest of the World', in Robert I. Rotberg (ed.) *China into Africa: Trade, Aid, and Influence*, Washington, DC: Brookings Institution Press, pp. 155–196.

Siddiqa, Ayesha (2020) 'Shia-Sunni Rift on Rise in Pakistan, but Imran Khan Govt's Silence May Be Strategic', *The Print*, 28 September. Available at: https://theprint.in/opinion/shia-sunni-rift-on-rise-in-pakistan-but-imran-khan-govts-silence-may-be-strategic/511942/ (accessed 30 April 2021).

Siddiqa, Ayesha (2007) *Military Inc.: Inside Pakistan's Military Economy*, London: Pluto Press.

Singh, Ajit (2020) 'The Myth of "Debt-Trap Diplomacy" and Realities of Chinese Development Finance', *Third World Quarterly*, Vol. 42, No. 2, pp. 239–253.

Small, Andrew (2015) *The China-Pakistan Axis: Asia's New Geopolitics*, New York: Oxford University Press.

Smith Finley, Joanne (2019) 'Securitization, Insecurity and Conflict in Contemporary Xinjiang: Has PRC Counter-Terrorism Evolved into State Terror?' *Central Asian Survey*, Vol. 38, No. 1, pp. 1–26.

Smith Finley, Joanne (2020) 'Why Scholars and Activists Increasingly Fear a Uyghur Genocide in Xinjiang', *Journal of Genocide Research*. Doi: 10.1080/14623528.2020.1848109.

Syed, Anwar Hussain (1974) *China and Pakistan: Diplomacy of an Entente Cordiale*, Amherst: University of Massachusetts Press.

Talbot, Ian (1998) *Pakistan: A Modern History*, London: Hurst & Co.

Tiezzi, Shannon (2014) 'Is the Kunming Knife Attack China's 9–11?' *The Diplomat*, 4 March. Available at: https://thediplomat.com/2014/03/is-the-kunming-knife-attack-chinas-9–11/ (accessed 15 April 2021).

United Nations Security Council (2011) 'Eastern Turkistan Islamic Movement', 7 April. Available at: www.un.org/securitycouncil/sanctions/1267/aq_sanctions_list/summaries/entity/eastern-turkistan-islamic-movement (accessed 16 April 2021).

Wong, Edward (2009) 'China Says Its Forces Killed 12 in Xinjiang', *New York Times*, 20 July. Available at: www.nytimes.com/2009/07/21/world/asia/21china.html (accessed 14 April 2021).

Xu, Shaomin, and Li Jiang (2020) 'The Emergence and Fallacy of "China's Debt-Trap Diplomacy" Narrative', *China International Studies*, No. 2, pp. 69–84.

Yeh, Emily T., and Elizabeth Wharton (2016) 'Going West and Going Out: Discourses, Migrants, and Models in Chinese Development', *Eurasian Geography and Economics*, Vol. 57, No. 3, pp. 286–315.

Yeung, Jessie, James Griffiths, and Nectar Gan (2021) 'The US Is Sanctioning Chinese Officials Over Alleged Abuse of Uyghurs in Xinjiang. Here's What You Need to Know', *CNN*, 25 March. Available at: https://edition.cnn.com/2021/03/24/china/xinjiang-uyghur-explainer-intl-hnk/index.html (accessed 16 April 2021).

Zhang, Weihong (2010) 'China's Cultural Future: From Soft Power to Comprehensive National Power', *International Journal of Cultural Policy*, Vol. 16, No. 4, pp. 383–402.

6 CPEC reconfigured

Learning lessons from Pakistan's 'game changer'

6.1 Introduction: a reconfigured narrative

The chapter begins with a summary of the findings in the book. The summary outlines the main points obtained from the analysis of CPEC's planning and implementation conducted in the preceding chapters, attempting to demonstrate what CPEC is and is not, drawing on the evidence. In other words, the most important aspects of the deconstruction and reconfiguration of CPEC conducted in the book are summarised. On the basis of the summary, I then attempt to draw out some lessons that can be learnt from the analysis concerning other BRI projects and 'economic corridors', as well as interstate connectivity projects in general. Next, I outline what would need to be done for CPEC to become truly a 'game changer' in the South Asian and Central Asian regions, and whether it is realistic to expect such developments. Finally, I draw some conclusions about what can be expected from CPEC in the coming years.

6.2 Summary of the findings

There are five key findings which emerge from the analysis conducted in this book. The first is that despite its name, the China-Pakistan Economic Corridor is not purely – or even primarily – a project motivated by economics. Geopolitical and security motivations are at the forefront of Chinese and Pakistani calculations concerning CPEC. Even if both sides do also hope for economic benefits from the megaproject, the twin goals of transforming Pakistan into an economic powerhouse – or at least setting the nation on a more stable footing – and increasing trade and overland connectivity between China and Pakistan are secondary to security-related aims.

The analysis in this book demonstrates that the primary drivers of consolidating cooperation between China and Pakistan via CPEC are (1) to counter the Indian presence in Kashmir, and (2) to suppress separatist elements within both China and Pakistan. These are the same primary drivers that have fuelled cooperation between China and Pakistan since the China-India War of 1962. In the long-term strategic calculations of Chinese and Pakistani elites, geopolitical and security goals thus override the officially stated economic and geo-economic aims

DOI: 10.4324/9781003018377-6

which are assumed by many scholars and other observers to be the main drivers of CPEC. The megaproject is not so much a 'game changer' as a 'cooperation consolidator', 'security stabiliser', and 'geopositional gambit'.

The second key finding is related to the first one. The analysis reveals the dominant role of Pakistan's civil-military elites in the running of CPEC. Although information is sparse, communication between the Pakistani and Chinese sides about CPEC appears, over the long term, to have involved backroom dialogue at the elite level, most probably involving at all stages representatives of the two parties' militaries. The chairman of the CPEC Authority until August 2021, Asim Saleem Bajwa, is a retired three-star general in the Pakistani army with a family business empire which grew in tandem with his rise through the military (Inayat 2020). In addition, since his rise to power in August 2018, Imran Khan has clearly struggled – like many a Pakistani prime minister before him – to take control of the CPEC discourse in the face of backroom manoeuvrings by civil-military elite elements. He is aware of the power of the military in Pakistan's governance, which, as this book has demonstrated, has frequently over the years seized power from democratically elected regimes. In one case, a deposed head of state – Zulfikar Ali Bhutto – ended up hanging from a gallows pole at the behest of the military commander who deposed him (Saeed et al 2014: 210). The point is that while such extreme measures are not now on the cards, the history of Pakistan demonstrates the weakness of elected heads of state and the power of the military in deciding long-term policy, including cooperation with China.

The evidence in this book has documented the fragility of the state of Pakistan, its internal separatist tendencies, and the role of the military in holding the state together. It has also demonstrated the key role of India in Chinese and Pakistani calculations concerning security and regional geopolitics. Despite protestations to the contrary, China has also obviously supported Pakistan's unending quest for military parity with India. In these circumstances, it is clearly the case that the military must be playing a prominent role in the planning and implementation of a key megaproject such as CPEC. The megaproject's focus on Chinese investments in Gwadar port, energy production, and transport infrastructure means that CPEC is designed not only to develop Pakistan's economy but also to consolidate the Pakistani civil-military elite's ability to sustain political power and achieve the twin security goals of pushing back against India and containing separatism in outlying regions of the country. The intense focus within Pakistan on the ML-1 rail connection from Karachi in Sindh to Lahore in Punjab and Peshawar in Khyber Pakhtunkhwa is indicative of a desire to ensure that as many as possible of Pakistan's key urban centres, which form the backbone of the country, are connected and accessible as needs demand.

The third key finding – known to many but still in need of emphasis – is that CPEC is focused overwhelmingly on projects within Pakistan rather than across the border with China. The only new cross-border infrastructure to be constructed since the advent of CPEC in 2015 is a fibre-optic cable. All the remaining projects planned and implemented are solely within Pakistan. On the official CPEC website there is no mention of any infrastructure projects on the Chinese side of the border as falling within the remit of CPEC (China-Pakistan Economic Corridor (CPEC) Official Website 2021). In addition, the development of Gwadar port, for which the Chinese have a 40-year lease, has been slow. The port's usage by maritime transport traffic has been surprisingly limited so far, meaning that its role to date in enhancing international connectivity has been minimal. Acknowledging CPEC's intra-Pakistan characteristics means that it is difficult to see it as having any implications for cross-border or regional connectivity as it has been planned and implemented so far. Most especially, it is unclear how a project that has not been implemented in Xinjiang province – to which, in the original conception, Gwadar port was supposed to be connected via the length of Pakistan by new transport and pipeline infrastructure – can be considered an international 'economic corridor' or regional 'game changer' in any meaningful sense. It could be argued that CPEC as it has been implemented so far is only in its early stages; however, in the apparent absence of any planned projects which involve Xinjiang apart from the already-constructed fibre-optic cable, and also given the surprisingly limited development and usage of Gwadar port so far, it is difficult to conclude that CPEC can be designated as anything more than an attempt, in part, to develop an intra-Pakistani economic corridor.

A fourth finding – related to the third one – concerns the transport and energy infrastructure construction projects within Pakistan which dominate China's CPEC investments, and for which feasibility and sustainability studies (if they exist) have not been made public: close scrutiny of details reveals a range of problems surrounding these projects. As Chapter 3 demonstrated, progress on these has been slower than expected, especially the transportation projects: this unexpectedly slow progress casts doubt on the 'game changer' narrative often advanced for CPEC. There are also concerns about sustainability, especially environmental sustainability. This point is especially relevant to CPEC's energy projects but is an issue which concerns all new infrastructure being constructed by Chinese companies. Whether construction activity involves dredging Gwadar port, building dams, laying down railways, or expanding coal mines, it would be preferable to ascertain the possible environmental impacts before beginning construction. However, it is difficult to find any evidence of environmental sustainability studies having been conducted in advance of CPEC infrastructure construction projects. It seems that environmental sustainability has not constituted one of the guiding principles of the megaproject. Indeed, as Table 6.1 demonstrates, Chinese scholars have only begun to take an interest in the environmental impacts of CPEC since 2017: none of the 20 Chinese-language publications published between 2013 and 2016 examined in the research for this book even mentioned environmental issues, whereas 5 out of 20 published from 2017 to 2019 discussed the possibility of negative environmental impacts. A conclusion can be drawn from the total absence of environmental sustainability studies and discussion of environmental sustainability in the Chinese-language scholarly literature prior to 2017 that awareness of the potential environmental impacts of CPEC construction projects was non-existent on the Chinese side at the time of the megaproject's launch.

Table 6.1 Scholars' analysis of environmental impacts

	Assume environmental sustainability	*Critically interrogate environmental sustainability*	*Environmental sustainability not mentioned*
English-language publications, 2015–2017 (30)	10% (3)	17% (5)	73% (22)
English-language publications, 2018–2020 (30)	3% (1)	30% (9)	67% (20)
Chinese-language publications, 2013–2016 (20)	0% (0)	0% (0)	100% (20)
Chinese-language publications, 2017–2019 (20)	0% (0)	25% (5)	75% (15)
All publications (100)	4% (4)	19% (19)	77% (77)

Source: author

Given the prevalence of coal mines, coal-powered energy plants, and hydropower projects in the list of CPEC projects (see Table 2.4), the lack of attention to environmental sustainability is obviously a concern. As some Chinese scholars have belatedly noticed, there is a high risk of negative impacts on Pakistan's environment resulting from CPEC construction projects (Shi et al 2017; Wang et al 2017). However, rigorous environmental studies remain in short supply.

The economic sustainability of CPEC projects is also obviously a concern. Even though some scholars have correctly critiqued worries about China's 'debt-trap diplomacy' as an over-extended media trope lacking substantiation (Brautigam 2020), there still remain serious questions in this case about how Pakistan will repay what it owes China for CPEC investments. The problem is compounded by lack of transparency about interest rates, as well as mandatory insurance payments to the Chinese state-funded policy insurer Sinosure: the latter are routinely required as part of China's overseas investment packages (Wolf 2020: 187–189). Since China necessitates taking out insurance with Sinosure as part of loan conditions, Sinosure effectively has a monopoly on this business. Sinosure insurance payments are also significant: according to a report in the Pakistani news outlet *Dawn*, Sinosure charges a fee of around 7 per cent for debt servicing. This fee is on top of interest, financing fees and charges, and capital repayment, pushing repayments on a single 660MW project at Port Qasim up from a capital cost of US$767.9 million to a total of US$956.1 million (Siddiqui 2015). Thus, even if China claims that interest rates on loans from state-backed financial institutions such as Exim Bank are lower than other international lenders, fees and insurance payments accumulate on top to make total repayments significantly higher than capital costs.

Given Pakistan's ever-growing trade deficit with China, and its perennial lack of liquidity in terms of foreign exchange reserves, it is difficult to see how it is going to finance its debts to China. There is also evidence that the Chinese have recognised this problem since they have been reluctant to add further loans to Pakistan's existing repayment burden (Aamir 2021). All these factors – Pakistan's lack of liquidity, Pakistan's accumulated debt to China, and Chinese reluctance to commit more funds given the inherent risks – are likely to slow down progress on CPEC projects in the coming years.

The final key takeaway of the analysis conducted in this book is that there are lessons to be learnt concerning the scholarly interpretation of official proclamations about megaprojects such as CPEC which involve cooperation between two states. Scholars and the media need to be careful about taking official proclamations at face value and continuing to transmit them to their audiences as if they were empirically verified facts. In the case of CPEC, there are various problematic aspects of the megaproject which demand verification, including some which cannot be verified at all – most notably the non-existent but frequently mentioned cross-border pipeline project analysed in Chapter 4. On the other hand, there is as yet no justification for designating CPEC or Gwadar as white elephants, because the projects underway will certainly have utility of one kind or another. In the case of Gwadar, the lack of progress with the commercial development of the port suggests that the rationale behind the Chinese presence is not purely economic – and, in fact, is more likely to relate to geostrategic and security goals connected to the Indian Ocean and protecting China's interests there. Most notable among these are the sea lines of communication through which pass a large percentage of China's supplies of energy and raw materials, as well as Chinese shipping on the way to and from Europe and Africa. It is for this reason that I posited in Chapter 4 that China's long-term interest in Gwadar can be classified as *geopositional hedging*: occupying – by legal means – a territory such as a port city with a view to its possible long-term utility as a geostrategic asset in the event of future need.

The evidence presented in this book demonstrates that it is essential to be careful to deconstruct official narratives, slogans, and oft-repeated tropes. It is not just in China-Pakistan relations that such tropes become established. Truisms and soundbites, propagated by modern media – but often also recycled by scholars – often tend to dominate discourse in many (if not all) countries. The broad propagation of easy-to-understand but unnuanced and often plain incorrect tropes tends to make discussion of foreign policy reproductive rather than analytical. Unfortunately, however, in the case of China-Pakistan relations and CPEC, such tropes seem to have stuck and become fixed over long periods of time, distorting perceptions, and pre-empting constructive critique. This book stands as a warning to observers everywhere of the need to deconstruct official narratives in order to be able to assemble a reconfigured picture of the situation which better corresponds to the empirical reality.

6.3 Questions of media freedom, academic quality, and corruption

At the end of this study, there remain many unanswered – or not fully answered – questions about CPEC. In part, this may be due to the limitations of this book and the omissions of the author, but unresolved issues are also caused by a lack of information – or selective information – emerging from Pakistan concerning certain aspects of the megaproject. Questions which have not been fully answered either in this book or in general include the following:

- Why do many scholarly studies of CPEC emerging from Pakistan tend to cleave so closely to the official line and accept it so uncritically? (This is also the case in some Chinese studies, but surprisingly some of them are more critical than one would expect: for instance, Zheng 2016; Yang and Tu 2018.)
- What precisely is the role of personal relations and/or corruption at the elite level in the implementation of CPEC?
- To what extent do suppression and control of information in Pakistan and China play a role in promoting official depictions of CPEC which continue to portray it as purely economic in character?

In each case, it is possible to draw some conclusions and make some suggestions concerning these questions. However, it is not possible to answer them fully. Fuller answers with greater empirical support will have to await further research beyond the scope of this study and the capabilities of the author.

First, it is possible to make some educated guesses as to why many English-language scholarly studies of CPEC, especially those originating in Pakistan, tend to lack sufficient critical perspective and tend to recycle official agendas. One reason could be the acknowledged low quality of the public education system in Pakistan: access to a high-quality education – including education in the English language – is generally restricted to elites and is closed to the children of less privileged classes (Manan and David 2014: 206–207). Dissenting voices from outside the elite classes therefore generally do not receive an education or a platform which would allow them to express their discontent: there are exceptions to this rule, but it should be stressed that they are indeed exceptions.

In connection with this point, in a country in which the children of elites both have a vested interest in system maintenance and are the most educated citizens with the best access to university positions, it is probable that voices critical of the status quo are not going to be abundant. Fear of reprisals is also a factor: as outlined in Chapter 5, Pakistan has a low-security environment in which acts of violent retaliation against dissenting voices (particularly those seen as un-Islamic) occur frequently. For instance, after the prominent politician Salman Taseer, a founder of the PPP and supporter of democracy and pluralism – including for non-Muslim minorities – was murdered in 2011, his assassin "was met by cheering crowds that showered him with flowers" (Ullah 2014: 2). Taseer had been a supporter of President Zulfiqar Ali Bhutto, who was hanged in 1979 after a military coup (Saeed et al 2014: 210). Hard-line Muslim clerics regarded Taseer's democratic vision as "tantamount to Westernization and the destruction of true Islam in Pakistan" (Ullah 2014: 2). Attacks on journalists – apparently including at least one by agents of the Pakistani military establishment – are reportedly also rife in today's Pakistan, which is ranked 145th on the World Press Freedom Index (Ellis-Petersen 2021; Mir 2021). In such an atmosphere of intolerance, scholars are less likely to espouse unconventional opinions – either those which contradict hard-line Muslims or the official line emanating from Pakistan's civil-military elites – for fear of reprisal than in countries with greater protection for freedom of speech and lower levels of sectarian and politically motivated violence.

A similar point, of course, might be said to be true for Chinese scholars publishing on CPEC who might be concerned about their security if they express opinions which differ from the official line. However, it is noticeable that there are critical voices among Chinese scholars publishing on CPEC (e.g. Zheng 2016; Yang and Tu 2018). Chinese scholars have discussed sensitive topics analysed in this book, such as the role of the Pakistani military elites in CPEC (Huang et al 2017) and the expansion of geopolitical influence through geographical location and geostrategic position (Zang and Zhu 2017). These are topics which are generally neglected by scholars located in Pakistan. Overall, the existence of more sceptical and probing Chinese studies of CPEC than Pakistani ones is probably indicative of the investment of Pakistani elites in the megaproject and the relative distance of the Chinese from what is essentially a set of Pakistan-based infrastructure projects utilising Chinese funds. Put simply: since CPEC is an elite-backed project taking place in Pakistan, Pakistani scholars have less room to criticise than Chinese scholars, who can justifiably take the position that they are examining risks to Chinese investments under the CPEC label. Pakistani scholars may argue that they also evaluate risks, but the analysis outlined in earlier chapters of this book reveals that many of these evaluations tend to be brief, incomplete, and lacking in sufficient rigour.

As far as the corruption question is concerned, in the absence of clear evidence this must remain unanswered. However, the scandal that erupted in 2020 around Asim Bajwa (then the chairman of the CPEC authority) concerning his family's business interests in the United States is indicative of the potential for future revelations. In addition, an August 2020 report in *Business Recorder* mentions accusations of former government ministers taking bribes to include specific projects in CPEC leading to "investigations which were later on shelved" (Ghumman 2020). It is therefore likely that corruption allegations are likely to dog the progress of CPEC into the future.

At any rate, it is difficult to deny that the management of Chinese investments in Pakistan under the CPEC label has been less transparent than international standards regarding investments would normally require. The lack of transparency and oversight in CPEC is already an acknowledged concern which was raised in 2020 by a senior US diplomat (Syed 2020). Given the evidence outlined in earlier chapters concerning collusion between Chinese and Pakistani civil-military elites in cooperation between the two countries, it would not be surprising if such collusion extended to the granting of contracts to preferred parties and similar activity. The record of Chinese investments in other parts of the world under the BRI label is not encouraging. For instance, there is the well-known CEFC case, in which the company's chief financial officer (Patrick Ho) was arrested and convicted in the United States for bribing African leaders (Lau 2020). The head of CEFC, Ye Jianming, has been detained in China since 2018 for reasons which have not been publicised, but which are almost certainly related to Ho's conviction and the failure of CEFC investments in the Czech Republic (Garlick 2019b: 444). The CEFC scandal attests to the potential for allegations of corruption to arise in connection with Chinese overseas investments, including CPEC.

Moving on to the third question about top-down control of agendas influencing the depiction of CPEC as purely economic in character, the close relationship between official pronouncements and scholarly or media coverage of CPEC can only be suggestive of a system in which top-down control of information channels is prevalent. In these circumstances, it is, in fact, surprising that there appear to be more dissenting voices concerning CPEC in the media than in academia. Journalists working at publications such as *Dawn* and *Business Recorder* have managed to publish some material which is critical of CPEC (e.g. Akhtar 2020; Ghumman 2020) even though the vast majority of articles are not critical. The fact that material has been uncovered and reported by journalists which is critical of the megaproject and the government's approach to cooperation with China only underlines the fact that there is an insufficient number of critical scholarly voices from within Pakistan.

6.4 Comparison of other BRI projects with CPEC

There is no space in this book to conduct a full-scale comparative study of CPEC in relation to Chinese investments in other economically developing countries under the umbrella of the BRI. Such research is much needed but is beyond the remit of this book: indeed, it would necessitate an entire book-length study, probably multi-authored. However, it is worth drawing out some salient points concerning CPEC and the BRI through some comparisons with other BRI projects. Specifically, it is possible to identify some common traits of Chinese investments which are present in Pakistan as well as in other countries.

Above all, there is the fact that Chinese investment deals are almost always negotiated bilaterally, with one partner country at a time. This is clear in the case of CPEC, where all projects not only have been sealed with Pakistan alone but are also located, as already demonstrated, almost solely inside Pakistan. Examining other Chinese foreign infrastructure investment projects reveals that there are some which include a multilateral aspect in that they involve more than one other country besides China. For instance, there is the Addis Ababa to Djibouti railway, which connects Ethiopia and Djibouti, or the gas pipelines from Turkmenistan to Xinjiang, which cross Uzbekistan and Kazakhstan (necessarily, otherwise they would not be able to reach China). However, most other Chinese foreign investment and infrastructure-building projects involve only China plus one other actor. It is for this reason that China is often accused of 'divide and conquer' tactics (Bolzen and Erling 2012; Garlick 2019a). So many Chinese investments are 'China + 1' that Chinese claims of seeking to operate through regional cooperation platforms such as '17 + 1' (in Central and Eastern Europe), the Forum on China-Africa Cooperation (FOCAC), or the China-Arab States Cooperation Forum (CASCF) tend to be undermined by the empirical reality. The role of Chinese-led multilateral cooperation frameworks is generally unclear, and in practice China tends to favour trade and investment negotiations at the bilateral rather than regional level.

The '17 + 1' regional platform for cooperation between China and Central and Eastern European (CEE) countries is a good illustration of this point. When initiated in 2012, it seemed as if the then '16 + 1' – Greece was added in 2019 (Ciurtin 2019) – was intended to generate multilateral intraregional synergies. However, meetings of the 17 + 1 take place only once per year and China persists in striking deals at the bilateral level, with individual countries and without reference to the 17 + 1 framework. Countries such as Lithuania and the Czech Republic have complained of clandestine Chinese influence attempts and unfulfilled promises of large-scale investment (Garlick 2019a). In May 2021, Lithuania withdrew from the 17 + 1, calling for it to be replaced by a '27 + 1' – meaning that the EU countries should act together in working out how to develop relations with China (Lau 2021). There is thus a mismatch between Chinese and local perceptions of how cooperation is supposed to work in the CEE region. There is also a mismatch between China's claim that it favours multilateral regionalism and the perceptions of some in Europe – for instance Lithuanian Foreign Minister Gabrielius Landsbergis – that China is using 'divide and conquer' tactics (Lo and Zheng 2021).

Like the 17 + 1, one of the selling points of CPEC was that it was supposed to transform Pakistan into a hub for regional economic cooperation by creating an 'economic corridor' connecting the Indian Ocean with Central Asia. However, as in the 17 + 1, the regional integration aspect of CPEC has largely been neglected as the largest part of Chinese investments have been concentrated on developing Pakistan's energy sector. Apart from a fibre-optic cable, no cross-border connectivity projects have been implemented so far. Thus, as is the case with 17 + 1, the regionalising aspect of CPEC has faded from view as China's investment activity has focused on projects within a single country – Pakistan – rather than regional, cross-border connectivity. With even the border between Pakistan and China consisting of a single official entry point which has not been noticeably enhanced over the duration of CPEC, there is as yet no sign that the Chinese are intending in practice to develop cross-border overland connections despite what the official rhetoric suggests.

The Belt and Road Initiative can be analysed in a similar way. Promoted as an initiative connecting countries together through new transportation infrastructure built using Chinese companies and Chinese funds, the BRI – and its 'economic corridors' – have not yet reached fruition due to the fact that China's definition of 'unimpeded trade' – promoted in official and semi-official BRI pronouncements – seems to consist of striking bilateral deals with individual countries rather than pursuing regional integration (Garlick 2020: 106). Peter Ferdinand points out that China's preference for striking bilateral deals leads "to weaker cross border integration than was intended in Europe, since it focuses upon creating shared transport links, while leaving the production structure in each country untouched" (Ferdinand 2016: 950). Countries also complain that when they open their markets to China, they do not obtain the equivalent level of access to Chinese markets. In the case of Pakistan, the widening trade gap analysed in Chapter 3 reveals that Islamabad is having similar problems to other BRI countries in that 'win-win' cooperation with China appears as if it will turn out to be a case (as per the oft-repeated joke) of 'China wins twice'.

The analysis of CPEC conducted in this book is therefore illustrative of the perception problems and practical issues generated by Chinese investments. By investing in Pakistan and other countries through bilateral agreements negotiated behind closed doors and containing financial terms which are not declared publicly, China makes itself an easy target for accusations of 'debt-trap diplomacy', 'divide and conquer', and 'neo-colonialism'. Even if studies have demonstrated that such accusations typically lack evidential foundations and are more akin to tropes than representations of reality (Garlick 2019a; Brautigam 2020), the perception remains that China is exploiting developing countries rather than assisting them.

Be this as it may, the imputation that China is trying to gain political influence in partner countries through infrastructure investment projects should be taken seriously. Political influence allows Beijing to achieve a range of goals: support for the One China policy, which dictates the non-recognition of Taiwan; votes supporting Chinese initiatives in the United Nations; ensuring supplies of raw materials for China's domestic economy; opening up new markets for Chinese companies; ensuring minimal or no support for Uyghur or Tibetan independence; increasing China's clout in the global South; and allowing Beijing to establish a Chinese presence in as many countries as possible as a form of strategic or geopositional hedging against future contingencies and risk. As in other countries included in the BRI, China's investments in Pakistan under the banner of its 'flagship project' CPEC allow Beijing to pursue all or most of those goals – with specific characteristics adapted to the case of Pakistan. Most notably, as the analysis in this book has demonstrated, China's foremost priorities in its partnership with Pakistan over the long term – and including CPEC – have a high degree of similarity to Pakistan's: countering India and ensuring the suppression of separatist elements within the nation.

6.5 Conclusion: CPEC into the future

The main argument of this book is that analysing the empirical record of CPEC reveals that geopolitics and security concerns tend to undermine official proclamations – and the assertions of scholars – that the megaproject is solely about economic development. Oft-repeated claims that CPEC will be a 'game changer' for Pakistan and solve China's 'Malacca dilemma' do not stand up under scrutiny. Merely repeating such assertions simply because they were made by the erstwhile leaders of one or the other partner does not make them true. Chinese investments in energy, transportation, and port infrastructure projects within Pakistan, often moving forward more slowly than expected, have not yet remotely transformed Pakistan into an 'economic corridor' connecting the Indian Ocean with Xinjiang and Central Asia – and most likely, if they continue in the same vein, never will.

So how could CPEC be a true regional 'game changer' linking together regional economies and transforming Pakistan into a trade corridor and regional hub? There are five policy points that would need to be implemented. The first is that CPEC would need to be planned and implemented with greater transparency. Second, there would need to be a focus on cross-border connectivity and multilateral cooperation rather than behind-doors deals at the bilateral level taking place in one country (Pakistan). Third, there would also have to be more attention to environmental and economic sustainability. Fourth, it would be necessary to listen to voices from outside national elites to ensure the participation of the minorities who are the citizens of key regions such as Balochistan and Khyber Pakhtunkhwa. And fifth, it would be advisable to loosen controls over movement and trade rather than maintaining or increasing them in order to encourage increased economic activity. These policies, if implemented, could help to fulfil the stated goals of the megaproject in the long term. It would not be easy to implement such policies; but doing so would be a true step in the direction of the transformation suggested by the 'game changer' slogan.

But the truth is that such transformative policies are not likely to be implemented because they do not suit those who are striking deals on either the Chinese or Pakistani sides. Elite and military interests are paramount in CPEC as in earlier manifestations of Sino-Pakistani cooperation. Thanks to consistent Chinese support, control of CPEC by Punjabi elites and the military is likely to continue, as a recent study has demonstrated (Boni and Adeney 2020: 464). Geopolitics overrides geo-economics in Beijing's strategic calculations, just as it does in Islamabad's. Concern about how to contain India preoccupies the leaders of both militaries and guides their strategic planning. Both sides also worry about separatism within their borders and calculate that CPEC will help them to clamp down on separatist elements. These calculations govern the two sides' strategic thinking and CPEC is a part of it. This situation is unlikely to change given the shared, dominant role that countering India and containing separatism play in both sides' policy.

Pakistan is economically weak. China is strong. There is an inherent asymmetry in their relations which gives China room to manoeuvre and the ability to prevaricate and delay as necessary. In the absence of other willing partners, Pakistan needs China, which makes its civil-military elites enthusiastic about the continuation of CPEC. At the same time, China is also short of reliable allies. Mutual suspicions continue to poison relations with neighbourhood giant India despite frequent half-hearted attempts at rapprochement. It suits China to continue cooperation with Pakistan, albeit perhaps not at the rapid speed Pakistan's elites would prefer. It also suits China to have a territorial foothold on the Indian Ocean, which it otherwise lacks. Despite the repeated repetition that China respects other nations' sovereignty and supports non-interference in the domestic affairs of other countries, it also suits Beijing to have a degree of influence in Pakistan's internal affairs via backroom discussions about CPEC investments and Gwadar port.

The analysis of CPEC in this book thus tells a tale of consolidation rather than game-changing transformation. It reveals that geopolitical and security goals of necessity undercut geo-economic ones for both partners. It reveals that the weaknesses of CPEC are similar to those of the Belt and Road Initiative as a whole. And it reveals that scholars should be careful not to take official proclamations at face value but to interrogate them as rigorously as possible. A reconfigured CPEC is still one which involves close cooperation between China and Pakistan, but it is not at all the type of cooperation that official statements and scholarly publications recycling 'game changer' and 'Malacca dilemma' tropes would lead one to believe.

References

Aamir, Adnan (2021) 'China and Pakistan Fall Out Over Belt and Road Frameworks', *Nikkei Asian Review*, 19 January. Available at: https://asia.nikkei.com/Spotlight/Belt-and-Road/China-and-Pakistan-fall-out-over-Belt-and-Road-frameworks (accessed 2 March 2021).

Akhtar, Aasim Sajjad (2020) 'Rent-a-State', *Dawn*, 24 January. Available at: www.dawn.com/news/1530222/rent-a-state (accessed 30 May 2021).

Bolzen, Stefanie, and Johnny Erling (2012) 'Divide, Conquer, Aim East: China Has a Sharp New European Trade Strategy', *Die Welt*, 11 November. Available at: https://worldcrunch.com/world-affairs/divide-conquer-aim-east-china-has-a-sharp-new-european-trade-strategy (accessed 29 May 2021).

Boni, Filippo, and Katharine Adeney (2020) 'The Impact of the China-Pakistan Economic Corridor on Pakistan's Federal System: The Politics of the CPEC', *Asian Survey*, Vol. 60, No. 3, pp. 441–465.

Brautigam, Deborah (2020) 'A Critical Look at Chinese "Debt-Trap Diplomacy": The Rise of a Meme', *Area Development and Policy*, Vol. 5, No. 1, pp. 1–14.

China-Pakistan Economic Corridor (CPEC) Official Website (2021) Available at: cpecinfo.com (accessed 25 May 2021).

Ciurtin, Horia (2019) 'The "16+1" Becomes the "17+1": Greece Joins China's Dwindling Cooperation Framework in Central and Eastern Europe', *China Brief*, Vol. 19, No. 10, pp. 18–23.

Ellis-Petersen, Hannah (2021) '"Worse Day by Day": Journalists Speak Out After Pakistani Vlogger Tortured', *The Guardian*, 2 June. Available at: www.theguardian.com/global-development/2021/jun/02/hamid-mir-journalists-speak-out-after-pakistani-vlogger-asad-toor-tortured (accessed 2 June 2021).

Ferdinand, Peter (2016) 'Westward ho – The China Dream and "One Belt, One Road": Chinese Foreign Policy Under Xi Jinping', *International Affairs*, Vol. 92, No. 4, pp. 941–957.

Garlick, Jeremy (2019a) 'China's Economic Diplomacy in Central and Eastern Europe: A Case of Offensive Mercantilism?' *Europe-Asia Studies*, Vol. 71, No. 8, pp. 1390–1414.

Garlick, Jeremy (2019b) 'China's Principal-Agent Problem in the Czech Republic: The Curious Case of CEFC', *Asia Europe Journal*, Vol. 17, No. 4, pp. 437–451.

Garlick, Jeremy (2020) *The Impact of China's Belt and Road Initiative: From Asia to Europe*, Abingdon, UK: Routledge.

Ghumman, Mushtaq (2020) 'Chinese Banks Reluctant to Fund CPEC Projects in Current Climate: Sources', *Business Recorder*, 26 August. Available at: www.brecorder.com/news/40014542 (accessed 30 May 2021).

Huang, He, Xu Xueying, and Chen Ciyu (2017) 'Political Risks and Risk Control for Chinese Enterprises in Pakistan: A Case Study of the China-Pakistan Economic Corridor' (中国企业在巴基斯坦投资的政治风险及管控 – 以中巴经济走廊为例, Zhongguo qiye zai bajisitan touzi de zhengzhi fengxian ji guankong – yi zhong ba jingji zoulang wei li), *Global Review* (国际展望, *Guoji zhanwang*), Vol. 9, No. 2, pp. 132–148.

Inayat, Naila (2020) 'Asim Bajwa's Dirty Money Is RAW Saazish in Imran Khan's Pakistan', *The Print*, 10 September. Available at: https://theprint.in/opinion/letter-from-pakistan/asim-bajwas-dirty-money-is-raw-saazish-in-imran-khans-pakistan/499389/ (accessed 30 April 2021).

Lau, Chris (2020) 'Disgraced Former Hong Kong Minister Patrick Ho Returns to City after Serving Jail Term in New York for African Bribery Plot', *South China Morning Post*, 9 June. Available at: www.scmp.com/news/hong-kong/law-and-crime/article/3088264/disgraced-former-hong-kong-minister-patrick-ho-returns (accessed 30 May 2021).

Lau, Stuart (2021) 'Lithuania Pulls Out of China's '17+1' Bloc in Eastern Europe', *Politico*, 21 May. Available at: www.politico.eu/article/lithuania-pulls-out-china-17-1-bloc-eastern-central-europe-foreign-minister-gabrielius-landsbergis/ (accessed 30 May 2021).

Lo, Kinling, and Sarah Zheng (2021) 'China Says "Isolated Incidents" Won't Stop Cooperation with Central and Eastern Europe After Lithuania Quits "17+1"', *South China Morning Post*, 24 May. Available at: www.scmp.com/news/china/diplomacy/article/3134674/china-says-isolated-incidents-wont-stop-cooperation-central (accessed 31 May 2021).

Manan, Syed Abdul, and Maya Khemlani David (2014) 'Mapping Ecologies of Literacy in Educational Setting: The Case of Local Mother Tongues Vis-à-Vis Urdu and English Languages in Pakistan', *Language and Education*, Vol. 28, No. 3, pp. 203–222.

Mir, Hamid (2021) 'Imran Khan Promised Us Press Freedom in Pakistan. Now Journalists Are Under Attack', *The Guardian*, 2 June. Available at: www.theguardian.com/commentisfree/2021/jun/02/imran-khan-press-freedom-pakistan-journalists (accessed 2 June 2021).

Saeed, Luqman, Shabib Haider Syed, and Roger P. Martin (2014) 'Historical Patterns of Terrorism in Pakistan', *Defense & Security Analysis*, Vol. 30, No. 3, pp. 209–229.

Shi, Guoqing, Zhang Ruilian, Peng Shengping, Wu Shang, and Tang Bing (2017) 'Environmental and Social Risks Evaluation of Overseas Investment Pertaining to China-Pakistan Economic Corridor' (中国一巴基斯坦经济走廊投资社会风险探究, Zhongguo-bajisitan jingji zoulang touzi shehui fengxian tanjiu), *Journal of Hohai*

University (Philosophy and Social Sciences Edition) (河海大学学报（哲学社会科学版）, *Hehai daxue xuebao (zhexue shehui kexue ban)*), Vol. 19, No. 1, pp. 59–64.

Siddiqui, Hussain Ahmad (2015) 'CPEC Projects: Status, Cost and Benefits', *Dawn*, 13 July. Available at: www.dawn.com/news/1194014 (accessed 30 May 2021).

Syed, Baqir Sajjad (2020) 'FO Defends CPEC After Alice Wells' Criticism', *Dawn*, 23 May. Available at: www.dawn.com/news/1559080 (accessed 30 May 2021).

Ullah, Haroon K. (2014) *Vying for Allah's Vote: Understanding Islamic Parties, Political Violence, and Extremism in Pakistan*, Washington, DC: Georgetown University Press.

Wang, Huizhi, Hui Zhifan, and Xu Hehe (2017) 'An Analysis of Ecological Environment Risk and Countermeasures Pertaining to China-Pakistan Economic Corridor Construction' ("中巴经济走廊"建设生态环境风险分析与应对策略, "Zhong ba jingji zoulang" jianshe shengtai huanjing fengxian fenxi yu yingdui celue), *Journal of Hohai University* (*(Philosophy and Social Sciences Edition)* (河海大学学报（哲学社会科学版）, *Hehai daxue xuebao (zhexue shehui kexue ban)*), Vol. 19, No. 1, pp. 65–68.

Wolf, Siegfried O. (2020) *The China-Pakistan Economic Corridor of the Belt and Road Initiative: Concept, Context and Assessment*, Cham, Switzerland: Springer.

Yang, Wenwu, and Tu Jing (2018) 'Evaluating Geo-Strategic Risks to the Construction of the China-Pakistan Economic Corridor' (中巴经济走廊建设的地缘风险评价研究, Zhong ba jingji zoulang jianshe di diyuan fengxian pingjia yanjiu), *South Asian Studies Quarterly* (南亚研究季刊, *Nanya yanjiu jikan*), No. 1, pp. 76–85.

Zang, Xiuling, and Zhu Xunmin (2017) 'China-Pakistan Economic Corridor: Strategic Value and Challenges' (中巴经济走廊的战略价值及面临的挑战, Zhong ba jingji zoulang de zhanlue jiazhi ji mianlin de tiaozhan), *International Perspective* (国际视野, *Guoji shiye*), No. 2, pp. 72–76.

Zheng, Gang (2016) 'The Risk Challenges of CPEC, an Analysis of Grand Strategy and Countermeasures' (中巴经济走廊的风险挑战、大战略思考及其对策建议, Zhong ba jingji zoulang de fengxian tiaozhan, da zhanlue sikao ji qi duice jianyi), *Pacific Journal* (太平洋学报, *Taipingyang xuebao*), Vol. 24, No. 4, pp. 89–95.

Appendix 1

For the purposes of assessing interpretations of the CPEC in the scholarly literature, a sample of 100 representative scholarly publications on the topic was selected for qualitative and qualitative content analysis. Of these, 60 were in English and 40 in Chinese. Of the 60 English-language publications, 30 were published between 2015 and 2017, and 30 were published between 2018 and 2020. Of the Chinese-language texts, 20 were published between 2013 and 2016, and 20 were published between 2017 and 2019. The division into equal-sized groups of publications was done to allow for analysis of the possibility that there might have been shifts in focus or assumptions over time, for instance due to new evidence coming to light.

The main criterion for selection of the publications was that they were among the most cited on Google Scholar and CNKI (the Chinese academic database). Publications were eliminated if CPEC was found to be not the main focus of the text or if the analysis was not primarily political or economic (for instance if it was about religion or had a scientific focus, such as measuring rainfall).

In the case of the hypothetical oil pipeline connection from Gwadar to Xinjiang, the content of the publications was qualitatively analysed and coded according to the following criteria.

1 Authors were deemed to have assumed that a pipeline was being planned from Gwadar to Xinjiang **(1) if they mentioned a plan for such a pipeline in at least one sentence**, and **(2) if they did not critically interrogate that assumption anywhere in the text.**
2 Authors who mentioned a Gwadar-Xinjiang pipeline connection were deemed to have assumed that such a pipeline was feasible, economically sustainable, or secure **if they did not interrogate its feasibility, economic sustainability, or security in at least one sentence. If they questioned these issues at least once, albeit briefly and incompletely, or even without conviction**, then the article was ***not*** assessed as uncritically assuming that the putative pipeline was feasible, economically sustainable, or secure.

The quantitative part of the content analysis involved a simple count of publications which contained the terms 'game changer' and 'Malacca'. The results of the content analysis are presented in Tables 1.1, 2.1, 2.2, 2.3, and 6.1 in Chapters 1, 2, and 6.

Alphabetical list of publications

English-language publications

Published 2015–2017

Abid, Massarrat, and Ayesha Ashfaq (2015) 'CPEC: Challenges and Opportunities for Pakistan', *Journal of Pakistan Vision*, Vol. 16, No. 2, pp. 142–169.

Adnan, Mubeen, and Fatima Bushra (2016) 'China-Pakistan Economic Corridor: A Road to Development and Its Challenges', *South Asian Studies*, Vol. 31, No. 2, pp. 609–624.

Ahmad, Muhammad Salman, Fahad Asmi, Madad Ali, Md. Mashiur Rahman, and Syed Mudasser Abbas (2017) 'China-Pakistan Economic Corridor: In the Context of "String of Pearl Strategy" ', *International Journal of Business and Social Research*, Vol. 7, No. 8, pp. 26–42.

Ali, Liaqat, Jianing Mi, Mussawar Shah, Sayed Jamal Shah, Salim Khan, and Kausar BiBi (2017) 'The Potential Socio-Economic Impact of China Pakistan Economic Corridor', *Asian Development Policy Review*, Vol. 5, No. 4, pp. 191–198.

Ali, Waheed, Li Gang, and Mohsin Raza (2016) 'China-Pakistan Economic Corridor: Current Developments and Future Prospect for Regional Integration', *International Journal of Research*, Vol. 3, No. 10, pp. 210–222.

Avais, Muhammad Abdullah, Saima Shaikh, Hakim Ali Mahesar, and Fehmida Memon (2016) 'China-Pak Economic Corridor: Social Analysis for Pakistan', *The Government: Research Journal of Political Science*, Vol. 5, No. 5, pp. 163–171.

Bhattacharjee, Dhrubajyoti (2015) *China Pakistan Economic Corridor (CPEC)*. Indian Council of World Affairs, Issue Brief, 12 May.

Boyce, Tucker (2017) *The China-Pakistan Economic Corridor: Trade Security and Regional Implications*, Sandia Report (January 2017), Livermore, CA: Sandia National Laboratories. Available at: https://documents.pub/document/the-china-pakistan-economic-corridor-trade-security-and-numerous-regional-economic.html (accessed 13 May 2021).

Chaziza, Mordechai (2016) 'China-Pakistan Relationship: A Game-Changer for the Middle East?' *Contemporary Review of the Middle East*, Vol. 3, No. 2, pp. 1–15.

Esteban, Mario (2016) *The China-Pakistan Economic Corridor: A Transit, Economic or Development Corridor?* Madrid: Elcano Royal Institute, 5 July. Available at: www.realinstitutoelcano.org/wps/portal/rielcano_en/contenido?WCM_GLOBAL_CONTEXT=/elcano/elcano_in/zonas_in/ari53-2016-esteban-china-pakistan-corridor-transit-economic-development (accessed 14 May 2021).

Hussain, Ejaz (2017) 'China-Pakistan Economic Corridor: Will It Sustain Itself?' *Fudan Journal of the Humanities and Social Sciences*, Vol. 10, pp. 145–159.

Hussain, Mubashar, Muhammad Ilyas, Kashif Mahmood, and Ahmad Awais (2017) 'Pragmatic Reality of China Pakistan Economic Corridor: Impacts on Economy and Logistics Industry of Pakistan', *Science International (Lahore)*, Vol. 29, No. 5, pp. 1073–1078.

Hussain, Zahid (2017) 'The China-Pakistan Economic Corridor and the New Regional Geopolitics', *Asie.Visions*, No. 94, June, Brussels: Institut français des relations internationals (Ifri). Available at: www.ifri.org/en/publications/notes-delifri/asie-visions/china-pakistan-economic-corridor-and-new-regional (accessed 15 May 2021).

Ibrar, Muhammad, Jianing Mi, Muhammad Rafiq, and Arodh Lal Karn (2016) *The China-Pakistan Economic Corridor: Security Challenges.* 2nd Asia-Pacific Management and Engineering Conference (APME 2016), pp. 71–76. ISBN: 9781605954349.

Irshad, Muhammad Saqib, Qi Xin, and Hamza Arshad (2015) 'One Belt and One Road: Dose China-Pakistan Economic Corridor Benefit for Pakistan's Economy?' *Journal of Economics and Sustainable Development*, Vol. 6, No. 24, pp. 200–207.

Javaid, Umbreen (2016) 'Strengthening Geo-Strategic Bond of Pakistan and China through Geo-Economic Configuration', *Pakistan Economic and Social Review*, Vol. 54, No. 1, pp. 123–142.

Khan, Aarish U. (2015) 'Pak-China Economic Corridor: The Hopes and Reality', *Regional Studies*, Vol. 33, No. 1, pp. 43–60.

Kugelman, Michael (2017) 'The China-Pakistan Economic Corridor: What It Is, How It Is Perceived, and Implications for Energy Geopolitics', in Erica Downs, Mikkal E. Herberg, Michael Kugelman, Christopher Len, and Kaho Yu (eds.) *Asia's Energy Security and China's Belt and Road Initiative*, Seattle: The National Bureau of Asian Research, NBR Special Report No. 68 (November), pp. 15–27.

Lim, Alvin Cheng-Hin (2017) 'The Moving Border of the China-Pakistan Economic Corridor', *Geopolitics*, Vol. 24, No. 2, pp. 487–502.

Qureshi, Asif H. (2015) 'China/Pakistan Economic Corridor: A Critical National and International Law Policy Based Perspective', *Chinese Journal of International Law*, Vol. 14, No. 4, pp. 777–799.

Rahman, Saif Ur and Zhao Shurong (2017) 'Analysis of Chinese Economic and National Security Interests in China-Pakistan Economic Corridor (CPEC) Under the Framework of One Belt One Road (OBOR) Initiative', *Arts and Social Sciences Journal*, Vol. 8, No. 4, pp. 1–7.

Ramachandran, Sudha (2015) 'China-Pakistan Economic Corridor: Road to Riches?' *China Brief*, Vol. 15, No. 15. Available at: https://jamestown.org/program/china-pakistan-economic-corridor-road-to-riches/ (accessed 14 May 2021).

Ramay, Shakeel Ahmad (2016) *China Pakistan Economic Corridor: A Chinese Dream Being Materialized Through Pakistan*, Sustainable Development Policy Institute (SDPI) Policy Brief, 28 February. Available at: https://think-asia.org/handle/11540/9286 (accessed 14 May 2021).

Ranjan, Alok (2015) *The China-Pakistan Economic Corridor: India's Options*, New Delhi: Institute of Chinese Studies, Occasional Paper No. 8 (31 May). Available at: www.icsin.org/publications/the-china-pakistan-economic-corridor-indias-options (accessed 15 May 2021).

Ritzinger, Louis (2015) *The China-Pakistan Economic Corridor: Regional Dynamics and China's Geopolitical Ambitions*, Seattle: National Bureau of Asian Research (NBR), 5 August. Available at: www.nbr.org/publication/the-china-pakistan-economic-corridor/ (accessed 14 May 2021).

Shaikh, Faheemullah, Qiang Ji, and Ying Fan (2016) 'Prospects of Pakistan-China Energy and Economic Corridor', *Renewable and Sustainable Energy Reviews*, Vol. 59, pp. 253–263.

Talwar, Shreya (2015) ***China-Pakistan Economic Corridor and Its Geopolitical Implications***, New Delhi: Centre for Air Power Studies (CAPS), 22 June. Available at: http://capsindia.org/files/documents/CAPS_Infocus_ST.pdf (accessed 13 May 2021).

Vats, Rishap (2016) ***China-Pakistan Economic Corridor: Energy and Power Play***, New Delhi: Institute of Chinese Studies, Analysis No. 43 (November 2016). Available at: www.icsin.org/uploads/2017/05/12/6f85a6dcbfe146d2e332da723 2ab1852.pdf (accessed 13 May 2021).

Wolf, Siegfried O. (2016) ***The China-Pakistan Economic Corridor: An Assessment of Its Feasibility and Impact on Regional Cooperation***, Brussels: South Asia Democratic Forum (SADF) Working Paper No. 1 (28 June). Available at: https://papers.ssrn.com/sol3/papers.cfm?abstract_id=2834599 (accessed 15 May 2021).

Zhang, Ruilian, Francis Andam, and Guoqing Shi (2017) 'Environmental and Social Risk Evaluation of Overseas Investment Under the China-Pakistan Economic Corridor', ***Environmental Monitoring and Assessment***, Vol. 189, No. 6, pp. 1–16 (article no. 253).

Published 2018–2020

Afzal, Samrana, and Anum Naseem (2018) 'China Pakistan Economic Corridor (CPEC): Challenges and Prospects', ***Pakistan Administrative Review***, Vol. 2, No. 1, pp. 209–222.

Ahmad, Sohail, Sadia Sohail, and Muhammad Rizwan (2018) 'China Pakistan Economic Corridor and the Complex Interdependence', ***Global Regional Review***, Vol. 3, No. 1, pp. 64–75.

Ahmed, Manzoor (2018) 'The Economics and Politics of China-Pakistan Economic Corridor and Balochistan', ***Regional Studies***, Vol. 36, No. 4, pp. 70–111.

Ahmed, Salik Uddin, Amjad Ali, Dileep Kumar, Muhammad Zeeshan Malik, and Abdul Hameed Memon (2019) 'China Pakistan Economic Corridor and Pakistan's Energy Security: A Meta-Analytic Review', ***Energy Policy***, Vol. 127, pp. 147–154.

Ahmed, Zahid Shahab (2019) 'Impact of the China-Pakistan Economic Corridor on Nation-Building in Pakistan', ***Journal of Contemporary China***, Vol. 28, No. 117, pp. 400–414.

Alam, Khalid Mehmood, Xuemei Li, and Saranjam Baig (2019) 'Impact of Transport Cost and Travel Time on Trade Under China-Pakistan Economic Corridor (CPEC)', ***Journal of Advanced Transportation***, Vol. 2019, article ID 7178507, pp. 1–16.

Ali, Murad (2018) 'Pakistan's Quest for Coal-Based Energy Under the China-Pakistan Economic Corridor (CPEC): Implications for the Environment', ***Environmental Science and Pollution Research***, Vol. 25, No. 3, pp. 31935–31937.

Ali, Murad (2020) 'China-Pakistan Economic Corridor: Prospects and Challenges', ***Contemporary South Asia***, Vol. 28, No. 1, pp. 100–112.

Ali, Yousaf, Zaeem Rasheed, Noor Muhammad, and Salman Yousaf (2018) 'Energy Optimization in the Wake of China Pakistan Economic Corridor (CPEC)', ***Journal of Control and Decision***, Vol. 5, No. 2, pp. 129–147.

Aon, Muhammad, Muhammad Amin, and Ayesha Akram (2019) 'China Pakistan Economic Corridor', ***Advances in Social Sciences Research Journal***, Vol. 6, No. 7, pp. 453–457.

Asif, Muhammad (2018) 'China-Pakistan Economic Corridor: Security Concern and Role of Gwadar Port Prospect for Regional Integration', *International Journal of Research*, Vol. 5, No. 20, pp. 1464–1476.

Azhar, Muhammad, Abdul Basit Khan, and Ali Shan Shah (2019) 'China Pakistan Economic Corridor: Opportunities and Considerations', *FWU Journal of Social Sciences*, Vol. 13, No. 2, pp. 63–74.

Bahoo, Salman, Sohail Saeed, M. Javed Iqbal, and Shahid Nawaz (2018) 'Role of China-Pakistan Economic Corridor in Pakistan's Trade, Investment, Energy, Infrastructure, and Stock Market', *Journal of Independent Studies and Research – Management, Social Sciences and Economics*, Vol. 16, No. 1, pp. 63–83.

Garlick, Jeremy (2018) 'Deconstructing the China-Pakistan Economic Corridor: Pipe Dreams Versus Geopolitical Realities', *Journal of Contemporary China*, Vol. 27, No. 112, pp. 519–533.

Hussain, Mehmood, and Ahmed Bux Jamali (2019) 'Geo-Political Dynamics of the China-Pakistan Economic Corridor: A New Great Game in South Asia', *Chinese Political Science Review*, Vol. 4, No. 3, pp. 303–326.

Ibrar, Muhammad, Jianining Mi, Muhammad Rafiq, and Liaqat Ali (2019) 'China-Pakistan Economic Corridor: Ensuring Pakistan's Economic Benefits', *Khazar Journal of Humanities and Social Sciences*, Vol. 22, No. 1, pp. 38–51.

Idrees, Rao Qasim, Rohimi Shapiee, and Haniff Ahamat (2018) 'Energy Cost Saving and Economic Prospective of China Pakistan Economic Corridor', *International Journal of Energy Economics and Policy*, Vol. 8, No. 6, pp. 217–226.

Kanwal, Shamsa, Ren Chong, and Abdul Hameed Pitafi (2019) 'China-Pakistan Economic Corridor Projects Development in Pakistan: Local Citizens Benefits Perspective', *Journal of Public Affairs*, Vol. 19, No. 1, pp. 1–12.

Khan, Shehryar, and Guijian Liu (2018) 'The China-Pakistan Economic Corridor (CPEC): Challenges and Prospects', *Area Development and Policy*, Vol. 4, No. 4, pp. 466–473.

Kousar, Shazia, Abdul Rehman, Mahwish Zafar, Kamran Ali, and Nadia Nasir (2018) 'China Pakistan Economic Corridor: A Gateway to Sustainable Economic Development', *International Journal of Social Economics*, Vol. 45, No. 6, pp. 909–924.

Makhdoom, Atif Shan, Aisha Bashir Shah, and Kiran Sami (2018) 'Pakistan on the Roadway to Socio-Economic Development: A Comprehensive Study of China Pakistan Economic Corridor (CPEC)', *The Government: Research Journal of Political Science*, Vol. 6, No. 6, pp. 37–46.

Malik, Ahmad Rashid (2018) 'The China-Pakistan Economic Corridor (CPEC): A Game Changer for Pakistan's Economy', in B.R. Deepak (ed.) *China's Global Rebalancing and the New Silk Road*, Singapore: Springer, pp. 69–83.

Mirza, Faisal Mehmood, Nishat Fatima, and Kafait Ullah (2019) 'Impact of China-Pakistan Economic Corridor on Pakistan's Future Energy Consumption and Energy Saving Potential: Evidence from Sectoral Time Series Analysis', *Energy Strategy Reviews*, Vol. 25, pp. 34–46.

Qian, Hongdao, Sonia Azam, and Hamid Mukhtar (2018) 'China Pakistan Economic Corridor: Legal Injunctions and Protection of Chinese Investment in Pakistan Under OBOR Initiative', *European Journal of Research in Social Sciences*, Vol. 6, No. 2, pp. 29–37.

Raza, Hasan, Ahmed Osama, and Samreen Hena (2018) 'China Pakistan Economic Corridor (CPEC): The Counter Balancer of Momentous Energy Crisis in Pakistan', *Advances in Social Sciences Research Journal*, Vol. 5, No. 7, pp. 172–180.

Saad, Ahmad, Guan Xinping, and Mariah Ijaz (2019) 'China-Pakistan Economic Corridor and Its Influence on Perceived Economic and Social Goals: Implications for Social Policy Makers', *Sustainability*, Vol. 11, No. 18, pp. 1–20.

Shafqat, Saeed, and Saba Shahid (2018) *China Pakistan Economic Corridor: Demands, Dividends and Directions*, Lahore: Centre for Public Policy and Governance.

Shah, Abdur Rehman (2018) 'How Does China-Pakistan Economic Corridor Show the Limitations of China's "One Belt One Road" Model', *Asia & the Pacific Policy Studies*, Vol. 5, No. 2, pp. 378–385.

Wolf, Siegfried O. (2018) 'China-Pakistan Economic Corridor (CPEC): Regional Cooperation in the Wider South Asian Region', in B.R. Deepak (ed.) *China's Global Rebalancing and the New Silk Road*, Singapore: Springer, pp. 85–100.

Zhang, Ruilian, Guoqing Shi, Yuanni Wang, Si Zhao, Shafiq Ahmad, Xiaochen Zhang, and Qucheng Deng (2018) 'Social Impact Assessment of Investment Activities in the China-Pakistan Economic Corridor', *Impact Assessment and Project Appraisal*, Vol. 36, No. 4, pp. 331–347.

Chinese-language publications

Published 2013–2016

Chen, Jidong, and Zhang Jianquan (2016) 'Location of China-Pakistan Economic Corridor in "One Belt and One Road" Construction' (中巴经济走廊在"一带一路"建设中的定位, Zhong ba jingji zoulang zai "yidai yilu" jianshe zhong de dingwei), *Journal of Xinjiang Normal University (Philosophy and Social Sciences)* (新疆师范大学学报（哲学社会科学版）, *Xinjiang shifan daxue xuebao (zhexue shehui kexue ban)*), Vol. 37, No. 4, pp. 125–133.

Chen, Lijun (2014) 'The Construction of China-Pakistan Economic Corridor' (中巴经济走廊建设前景分析, Zhong ba jingji zoulang jianshe qianjing fenxi), *Research on Indian Ocean Economy* (印度洋经济体研究, *Yinduyang jingji ti yanjiu*), No. 1, pp. 107–121.

Cheng, Yunjie (2015) 'Sino-Pak Economic Corridor and Bilateral Trade Development' (中巴经济走廊背景下提升中巴贸易发展问题研究, Zhong ba jingji zoulang Beijing xia tisheng zhong ba maoyi fazhan wenti yanjiu), *South Asian Studies Quarterly* (南亚研究季刊, *Nanya yanjiu jikan*), No. 2, pp. 94–101.

Gao, Huiping (2014) 'Analysis on the Risk of Pakistan in the Construction of China-Pak Economic Corridor' (中巴经济走廊建设中的巴基斯坦风险分析, Zhong ba jingji zoulang jianshe zhong de bajisitan fengxian fenxi), *Southeast Asia and South Asia Studies* (东南亚南亚研究, *Dongnanya nanya yanjiu*), No. 1, pp. 64–68.

Gao, Zhigang, and Zhang Yan (2015) 'A Study of Bilateral Trade Potential and Efficiency in the Construction of China-Pakistan Economic Corridor – Based on Stochastic Frontier Gravity Model' (中巴经济走廊建设中双边贸易潜力及效率研究 – – 基于随机前沿引力模型分析, Zhong ba jingji zoulang jianshe zhong shuangbian maoyi qianli ji xiaolu yanjiu – jiyu suiji qianyan yinli moxing fenxi), *Financial and Economic Sciences* (财经科学, *Caijing kexue*), No. 11, pp. 332, 101–110.

He, Shiyou, and Xiao Xin (2015) 'Investment Risks of Energy and Power Projects in the China-Pakistan Economic Corridor' ("中巴经济走廊"能源电力项目的投资风险, "Zhong ba jingji zoulang" nengyuan dianli xiangmu di touzi fengxian),

International Economic Cooperation (国际经济合作, *Guoji jingji hezuo*), No. 2, pp. 82–85.

Li, Huiling, and Ma Haixia (2016) 'Pakistan's Economic Development Opportunities and the "Belt and Road" Construction' (巴基斯坦经济发展机遇与"一带一路"建设, Bajisitan jingji fazhan jiyu yu "yidai yilu" jianshe), *Academic Exploration* (学术探索, *Xueshu tansuo*), No. 7, pp. 36–43.

Li, Li, and Su Xin (2015) 'The Impact of Pakistan's Security Situation on the Construction of China-Pakistan Economic Corridor' (巴基斯坦安全形势对中巴经济走廊建设的影响, Bajisitan Anquan xingshi dui zhong ba jingji zoulang jianshe de yingxiang), *International Economic Cooperation* (国际经济合作, *Guoji jingji hezuo*), No. 5, pp. 17–21.

Li, Qingyan (2013) 'China-Pakistan Economic Corridor: A New Starting Point for Pragmatic Cooperation' (中国 – 巴基斯坦经济走廊：务实合作新起点, Zhongguo-bajisitan jingji zoulang: wushi hezuo xin qidian), *Contemporary World* (当代世界, *Dangdai shijie*), No. 9, pp. 51–53.

Liu, Zongyi (2015) 'Latest Progresses, Problems and Solutions of the "Belt and Road" Initiative in Southeast and Southwest Periphery of China' (我国"一带一路"倡议在东南、西南周边的进展现状、问题及对策, Woguo "yidai yilu" changyi zai dongnan, xinan zhoubian de jinzhan xianzhuang, wenti ji duice), *Indian Ocean Economic Studies* (印度洋经济体研究, *Yinduyang jingji ti yanjiu*), No. 4, pp. 92–109.

Liu, Zongyi (2016) 'Construction of the China-Pakistan Economic Corridor: Progress and Challenges' (中巴经济走廊建设：进展与挑战, Zhong ba jingji zoulang jianshe: jinzhan yu tiaozhan), *Research on International Issues* (国际问题研究, *Guoji wenti yanjiu*), No. 3, pp. 122–136.

Meng, Liaokuo (2015) 'Pakistan's Strategic Position from the Perspective of "One Belt One Road": Analysis of Its Realisation Path' ("一带一路"视野下的巴基斯坦战略地位及其实现路径探析, "Yidai yilu" shiye xia de bajisitan zhanlue diwei ji qi shixian lujing tanxi), *Forum of World Economics & Politics* (世界经济与政治论坛, *Shijie jingji yu zhengzhi luntan*), No. 4, pp. 30–45.

Niu, Biao (2014) 'Analysis of China-Pakistan Economic Corridor' (中巴经济走廊探析, Zhong ba jingji zoulang tanxi), *Open World* (开放世界, *Kaifang shijie*), No. 4, pp. 38–39.

Wang, Weihua (2015) 'The New Situation of South Asian Geopolitics and Its Impact on the Construction of China-Pakistan Economic Corridor' (南亚地缘政治新态势及其对中巴经济走廊建设的影响, Nanya diyuan zhengzhi xin taishi ji qi dui zhong ba jingji zoulang jianshe de yingxiang), *Research on Indian Ocean Economy* (印度洋经济体研究, *Yinduyang jingji ti yanjiu*), No. 4, pp. 57–73.

Yao, Yuanmei (2015) 'The Black Hole in the Afghanistan-Pakistan Border and the Difficulties of the Route Planning of China-Pakistan Economic Corridor' (阿巴边界"黑洞"与中巴经济走廊的路线困境, A ba bianjie "heidong" yu zhong ba jingji zoulang de luxian kunjing), *Arab World Studies* (阿拉伯世界研究, *Alabo shijie yanjiu*), No. 5, pp. 36–52.

Yao, Yun (2015) 'China-Pakistan Economic Corridor: A Risk Analysis' (中巴经济走廊面临的风险分析, Zhong ba jingji zoulang mianlin de fengxian fenxi), *South Asia Research* (南亚研充, *Nanya yan chong*) No. 2, pp. 35–45.

Yuan, Jianmin (2015) 'The Strategic Significance and Countermeasures of China-Pakistan Economic Corridor' (中巴经济走廊的战略意义及应对策略, Zhong ba jingji zoulang de zhanlue yiyi ji yingdui celue), *Xinjiang Social Science Forum* (新疆社科论坛, *Xinjiang she ke luntan*), No. 1, pp. 25–36.

Zhang, Chaozhe (2014) 'Building of China-Pakistan Economic Corridor: Opportunities and Challenges' (中巴经济走廊建设: 机遇与挑战, Zhong ba jingji zoulang jianshe: jiyu yu tiaozhan), *South Asian Studies Quarterly* (南亚研究季刊, *Nanya yanjiu jikan*), No. 2, pp. 79–103.

Zhang, Yuan (2016) 'How Do Balochistan Separatist Forces View China-Pakistan Economic Corridor and Why' (俾路支分离主义势力对中巴经济走廊的看法及其成因, Bi luz hi fenli zhuyi shili dui zhong ba jingji zoulang de kanfa ji qi chengyin), *South Asia Research* (南亚研充, *Nanya yan chong*) No. 2, pp. 24–42.

Zheng, Gang (2016) 'The Risk Challenges of CPEC, an Analysis of Grand Strategy and Countermeasures' (中巴经济走廊的风险挑战、大战略思考及其对策建议, Zhong ba jingji zoulang de fengxian tiaozhan, da zhanlue sikao ji qi duice jianyi), *Pacific Journal* (太平洋学报, *Taipingyang xuebao*), Vol. 24, No. 4, pp. 89–95.

Published 2017–2019

Chen, Jiyong, and Li Jurui (2019) 'Trade Potential and Its Influencing Factors on the Neighbouring Countries of the China-Pakistan Economic Corridor' ("中巴经济走廊"周边国家贸易潜力及其影响因素, "Zhong ba jingji zoulang" zhoubian guojia maoyi qianli ji qi yingxiang yinsu), *Research on Economics and Management* (经济与管理研究, *Jingji yu guanli yanjiu*), Vol. 40, No. 1, pp. 14–28.

Chen, Lijun (2017) '"One Belt One Road" and China-Pakistan Economic Corridor Construction' ("一带一路"与中巴经济走廊建设, "Yidai yilu" yu zhong ba jingji zoulang jianshe), *Contemporary World* (当代世界, *Dangdai shijie*), No. 1, pp. 54–57.

Chen, Lijun, and Liu Man (2017) 'Production Capacity Cooperation Against the Background of China-Pakistan Economic Corridor Construction' (中巴经济走廊建设背景下的产能合作, Zhong ba jingji zoulang jianshe beijing xia de channeng hezuo), *Social Sciences in Yunnan* (云南社会科学, *Yunnan shehui kexue*), No. 2, pp. 70–76.

Cheng, Yunjie, and Jiang Ruirui (2017) 'Complementarity and Competition of Commodity Trade Between China and Pakistan: Based on the Perspective of "China-Pakistan Economic Corridor" Construction' (中国与巴基斯坦商品贸易互补性和竞争性研究 – 基于"中巴经济走廊"建设视角, Zhongguo yu bajisitan shangpin maoyi hubu xing he jingzheng xing yanjiu – jiyu "zhong ba jingji zoulang" jianshe shijiao), *Journal of Xinjiang University (Philosophy, Humanities and Social Science)* (新疆师范大学学报（哲学社会科学版）, *Xinjiang shifan daxue xuebao (zhexue shehui kexue ban)*), Vol. 45, No. 3, pp. 1–8.

Huang, He, Xu Xueying, and Chen Ciyu (2017) 'Political Risks and Risk Control for Chinese Enterprises in Pakistan: A Case Study of the China-Pakistan Economic Corridor' (中国企业在巴基斯坦投资的政治风险及管控 – 以中巴经济走廊为例, Zhongguo qiye zai bajisitan touzi de zhengzhi fengxian ji guankong – yi zhong ba jingji zoulang wei li), *Global Review* (国际展望, *Guoji zhanwang*), Vol. 9, No. 2, pp. 132–148.

Li, Jianjun, and Sun Hui (2017) 'The Development of the China-Pakistan Economic Corridor in the Context of the Belt and Road Initiative: Present Basis and Path Selection' ("一带一路"背景下中巴经济走廊建设：现实基础与路径选择, "Yidai yilu" beijing xia zhong ba jingji zoulang jianshe: xianshi jichu yu lujing xuanze), *Journal of Xinjiang University (Philosophy, Humanities & Social Science)* (新疆大学学报（哲学·人文社会科学版）, *Xinjiang shifan daxue xuebao (zhexue shehui kexue ban)*), Vol. 45, No. 1, pp. 1–9.

Liang, Jenmin (2018) 'Construction of the China-Pakistan Economic Corridor: Significance, Progress and Path' (中巴经济走廊建设: 意义、进展与路径研究, Zhong ba jingji zoulang jianshe: yiyi, jinzhan yu lujing yanjiu), *Asia-Pacific Economy* (亚太经济, *Yatai jingji*), No. 5, pp. 13–20.

Ma, Bei (2018) 'China-Pakistan Relations Under the Framework of "One Belt One Road": Research on Security Risk Prevention' ("一带一路"框架下中国- 巴基斯坦: 安全风险防范研究, "Yidai yilu" kuangjia xia zhongguo-bajisitan: Anquan fengxian fangfan yanjiu), *World Religious Cultures* (世界宗 教 文化, *Shijie zongjiao wenhua*), No. 3, pp. 29–34.

Shi, Guoqing, Zhang Ruilian, Peng Shengping, Wu Shang, and Tang Bing (2017) 'Environmental and Social Risks Evaluation of Overseas Investment Pertaining to China-Pakistan Economic Corridor' (中国一巴基斯坦经济走廊投资社会风险探究, Zhongguo-bajisitan jingji zoulang touzi shehui fengxian tanjiu), *Journal of Hohai University (Philosophy and Social Sciences Edition)* (河海大学学报（哲学社会科学版), *Hehai daxue xuebao (zhexue shehui kexue ban)*), Vol. 19, No. 1, pp. 59–64.

Wang, Huizhi, Hui Zhifan, and Xu Hehe (2017) 'An Analysis of Ecological Environment Risk and Countermeasures Pertaining to China-Pakistan Economic Corridor Construction' ("中巴经济走廊"建设生态环境风险分析与应对策略, "Zhong ba jingji zoulang" jianshe shengtai huanjing fengxian fenxi yu yingdui celue), *Journal of Hohai University* (*(Philosophy and Social Sciences Edition)* (河海大学学报（哲学社会科学版), *Hehai daxue xuebao (zhexue shehui kexue ban)*), Vol. 19, No. 1, pp. 65–68.

Wang, Qi, and Mei Jianming (2017) 'Analyzing and Responding to Terrorist Threats Along the China-Pakistan Economic Corridor' (中巴经济走廊沿线恐怖威胁分析及对策威胁分析及对策, Zhong ba jingji zoulang yanxian kongbu weixie fenxi ji duice weixie fenxi ji duice), *South Asia Research* (南亚研充, *Nanya yan chong*), No. 4, pp. 15–41.

Wang, Qianting (2017) 'How to Correctly Lead the "Belt and Road": The Example of the China-Pakistan Economic Corridor' (如何正确引领"一带一路"的 – 以中巴经济走廊项目为例, Ruhe zhengque yinling "yidai yilu" de – yi zhong ba jingji zoulang xiangmu wei li), *Broadcasting & Television* (广电聚焦, *Guangdian jujiao*), No. 1, pp. 39–41.

Yan, Shigang (2017) 'Cooperation Strategy Between China and Pakistan Under "One Belt and One Road"' ("一带一路"下深化中国与巴基斯坦合作策略研究, "Yidai yilu" xia Shenhua zhongguo yu bajisitan hezuo celue yanjiu), *Reformation & Strategy* (改革与战略, *Gaige yu zhanlue*), Vol. 33, No. 5, pp. 36–39.

Yang, Wenwu, and Tu Jing (2018) 'Evaluating Geo-Strategic Risks to the Construction of the China-Pakistan Economic Corridor' (中巴经济走廊建设的地缘风险评价研究, Zhong ba jingji zoulang jianshe di diyuan fengxian pingjia yanjiu), *South Asian Studies Quarterly* (南亚研究季刊, *Nanya yanjiu jikan*), No. 1, pp. 76–85.

You, Hongbing, and Zhou Zhenzhen (2019) 'China-Pakistan Economic Corridor: A New Hub to Promote Comprehensive Regional Cooperation' (中巴经济走廊: 推动区域全面合作的新枢纽, Zhong ba jingji zoulang: tuidong quyu quanmian hezuo de xin shuniu), *International Economic Cooperation* (国际经济合作, *Guojia jingji hezuo*), No. 2, pp. 60–69.

Zang, Xiuling, and Zhu Xunmin (2017) 'China-Pakistan Economic Corridor: Strategic Value and Challenges' (中巴经济走廊的战略价值及面临的挑战, Zhong ba jingji zoulang de zhanlue jiazhi ji mianlin de tiaozhan), *International Perspective* (国际视野, *Guoji shiye*), No. 2, pp. 72–76.

Zhang, Jie, and Xu Rui (2018) 'An Analysis of Pakistan's Contribution to the "China-Pakistan Economic Corridor": Position and Countermeasures' (试析巴基斯坦对"中巴经济走廊"的:立场及对策, Shi xi bajisitan dui "zhong ba jingji zoulang" de: lichang ji duice), *Contemporary World* (当代世界, *Dangdai shijie*), No. 1, pp. 34–37.

Zhang, Xinping, and Zhang Liguo (2018) 'The Baluchistan Issue in the Construction of the China-Pakistan Economic Corridor' (中巴经济走廊建设中的俾路支问题, Zhong ba jingji zoulang jianshe zhong de bi luz hi wenti), *Peace and Development* (和平與發展, Heping yu fazhan), No. 5, pp. 33–49.

Zhang, Yaoming (2019) 'Construction of China-Pakistan Economic Corridor: Results, Risks and Countermeasures' (中巴经济走廊建设：成果、风险与对策, Zhong ba jingji zoulang jianshe: chengguo, fengxian yu duice), *Journal of Northwest University (Philosophy and Social Sciences Edition)* (西北大学学报（哲学社会科学版）, *Xibei daxue xuebao (zhexue shehui kexue ban)*), Vol. 49, No. 4, pp. 14–22.

Zhao, Jie, and Liu Ning (2017) 'The Impact of the China-Pakistan Economic Corridor on Chinese Trade: A Counterfactual Analysis Based on Industry Level Data from Belt and Road Countries' (中巴经济走廊贯通对中国进出口贸易的影响 – – 基于沿线国家产业层面数据的反事实模拟, Zhong ba jingji zoulang guantong dui zhongguo jin chukou maoyi de yingxiang – jiyu yanxian guojia chanye cengmian shuju de fan shishi moni), *World Economic Research* (世界经济研究, *Shijie jingji yanjiu*), No. 3, pp. 123–133.

Index

Page number in *italics* denote tables, those in **bold** denote figures